3000 IDIOMS AND PHRASES

3000 IDIOMS AND PHRASES

Sam Phillips

GOODWILL PUBLISHING HOUSE
B-9, Rattan Jyoti, 18, Rajendra Place
New Delhi-110008 (INDIA)

Published by
Rajneesh Chowdhry
for
Goodwill Publishing House
B-9, Rattan Jyoti
18, Rajendra Place
New Delhi-110008
Tel. : 5750801, 5755519
Fax : 91-11-5763428

Price : **Rs. 60/-**

Typeset at
Radha Laserkraft
R-814, New Rajinder Nagar
New Delhi-110060 • Tel. : 5730031

Printed at Kumar Offset Printers, Delhi-31

A-1

A-1 — (*very good, first rate*). He has done a wonderful job — it is really A-1.

ABC — (*elementary knowledge*). An arts student hardly knows ABC of science.

Abide

Abide by — (*to conform to*). One should abide by rules.

Abortive

Abortive effort — (*labour without success*). It is better to be successful in one game than to make abortive effort in all games.

Abound

Abound with, in — (*to be in plenty*). This pond abounds in fish. Forests abound with wild beasts.

About

Out and about — (*resorted to normal activity*). After a long illness my father is at last out and about.

To hang about — (*to stick around like a slave*). Many a men hang about the superintendent in Government offices.

To be put about — (*to be distracted*). All of us were much put about because of our manager's indisposition for a pretty long time.

To be dotted about — (*to be found everywhere*). Fifth columnists are dotted about India.

To come about — (*to take place*). Whatever may come about, I must get first division in my final examination.

To bring about — (*to cause to happen*). Only a revolution in the country can bring about a change in the existing circumstances.

To go about — (*to move from place to place*). You must stick to one job, going about jobs will not pay you in the long run.

Beat about or beat about the bush — (*indirect means to reach a thing*). Do not beat about the bush, be clear and frank.

Above

Above ground — (*alive*). Every Indian could trust Pandit Nehru when he was above ground.

Above all — (*before everything else*). He is very gentle and honest, but, above all, he is very hardworking.

Above criticism — (*without fault*). No human being is above criticism.

Above one's station — (*beyond one's position*). He may try his best but the post is definitely above his station.

Above board — (*frank and fair*). The main cause of his early success in business is his being above board.

To live above one's means — (*to spend more than one's income*). It is not wise to live above one's means.

Above one's understanding — (*that which is not easily understandable*). His talk is always above one's understanding.

Over and above — (*in addition to*). Over and above this problem, I want to discuss some other problems too.

Abroad

From abroad — (*from a foreign country*). Many people are coming from abroad day by day to see India.

Absence

Absence of mind — (*obstruction of thought*). He could not do well in examinations on account of absence of mind.

Absent

Absent-minded — (*to be inattentive*). An absent-minded student is never successful.

Absolute

A captain absolute — (*a self-willed person*). In a democratic government, a leader cannot afford to become a captain absolute; he has also to look to the other man's point of view.

Absorb

Absorb in — (*engrossed in*). When I reached home I found my brother absorbed in his studies.

Abstain

Abstain from — (*refrain from*). You should abstain from drinking.

Abstract

To abstract a thing from — (*to withdraw, to take out*). I have abstracted every penny from my bank account.

Abundance

Abundance of the heart — (*overflowing emotion*). Mahatma Gandhi supported the cause of Harijans with abundance of the heart.

Accede

Accede to — (*accept*). He had no way except to accede to my request.

Accept

Accept one's hand of friendship — (*to be friendly to each other*). India has always accepted a hand of friendship from every country.

Acceptable to — (*agreeable to*). The terms quoted by you are acceptable to me.

Acceptance

Acceptance — The acceptance of our proposals from Messrs Parry & Co. have duly been received.

Access

Access to — (*approach to*). Even his access to the Director could not get any job to Satish.

Accommodate

Accommodate to — (*to adjust*). A wise man always accommodates himself to his circumstances.

Accomplish

Accomplished in — (*skilled in*). Raju is accomplished in singing.

Accord

With one accord — (*with full agreement*). Election of Shri Lal Bahadur Shastri as India's second Prime Minister was with one accord of the Congress Party.

Of one's own accord — (*willingly*). He did everything of his own accord.

Accordance

In accordance with — (*in a manner consistent with*). To do things in accordance with law is always a wise thing.

According

According to — (*in conformity with*). Children should act according to the advice of their parents.

Account

Account for — (*explain*). You will have to account for your negligence.

On account — (*in part payment*). A cheque for Rs. 200/- from Messrs Girdharilal & Co. is received on account, the balance will be received in due course.

On one's account — (*on one's own risk responsibility*). I may remind you once again that everything you are doing is entirely on you own account.

To turn to account — (*to use for the best*). Wise men turn to account even their misfortunes.

To be accounted — (*to be esteemed*). Chanakya was accounted highly in the court of Ashoka.

To close an account with — (*to close financial dealings*). We have closed our account with the Punjab National Bank.

To open an account with — (*to start financial dealings*). We have opened an account with the Syndicate Bank.

To account for — (*to explain*). You will have to account for your behaviour at the meeting.

To square up an account — (*to clear an account*). By the payment of Rs. 400/- to us your accounts will be squared up fully.

To hold to no account — (*to hold in disrespect*). Suneeta holds her English teacher to no account.

To bring to account — (*to hold responsible*). People in India brought Mr. Krishna Menon to account for China's attack in 1962.

To go one's account — (*to die*). One day everybody will go to his account.

The great account — (*the day of judgement*). Only to the great account, the world can save it from a war.

Ace

Within an ace of — (*narrowly*). After the motor accident he escaped within an ace of death.

Acquaint

To be acquainted with — (*to be familiar*). He is acquainted with all the details of the problem.

Acquit

To acquit oneself of — (*to discharge*). One should acquit oneself of one's duties as best as possibly one can.

Across

To put it across — (*to get even with, to impose*). Thieves put it across the police and ran away.

To come across — (*to meet*). When you go to a hill-station you will come across a number of tunnels.

Act

To act — (*to behave*). Students are taught to act properly in schools.

To act on — (*to affect*). Cigarette acts on the mind.

To act upon — (*to obey*). It always pays to act upon the advice of elders.

Act of God — (*untoward happenings beyond the control of human forces*). Earthquake is an act of God.

To act up to — (*to put into practice*). Social institutions preach us to act up to noble ideas.

Action

To put in action — (*to practice*). If the Indian plans were put in action to the extent they are on paper, the economy of India would improve to a great extent.

Man of action — Lal Bahadur Shastri was a man of action.

Adam

Old as Adam — (*known from the earliest time*). There are a large number of historical places in India which are as old as Adam.

Adam's ale — (*water*). Please get me a glass of Adam's ale.

Not known from Adam — (*have no knowledge of; have never heard of*). I have not known from Adam your friend Mr. Kapoor.

Add

To add fuel to the fire — (*incite to worsen matters*). Samuel's way of speech always adds fuel to the fire.

To add insult to injury — (*to harm as well as insult*). An abuse always adds insult to injury.

Addict

Addicted to — (*accustomed; habituated — used in bad sense only*), Suresh is addicted to drinking.

Addle

Addle-headed — (*foolish*). Many collegians are addle-headed these days.

Addle-egg — (*proud*). My father-in-law is an addle-egg.

Adhere

Adhere to — (*to stick to*). One should adhere to one's principles.

Ad Hoc

Ad hoc — (*formed for one subject only*). From time to time ad hoc committees are formed to examine the cost of living in the country.

Adieu

To bid adieu — (*to take leave*). As the train whistled out, I bade him adieu.

Ado

Much ado about nothing — (*too much noise about small thing*). Parliamentarians generally make much ado about nothing.

Earning a few paise after a day's hard work is much ado about nothing.

Advance

Advance in life — (*growing old*). As a man advances in life he becomes more serious and conscious.

Advantage

To take advantage of — (*to avail oneself of*). You can take advantage of my influence for getting a job in Parry & Co.

To have advantage over — (*to be in a better position*). An employer has always many advantages over his employees.

Advantage ground — (*superiority in place or position*). Once a man gets popular, he is on advantage ground to go ahead with his schemes at a quick pace.

To take a person at an advantage — (*to catch one by surprise*). The Russians took the Americans at an advantage at the Geneva Conference.

Ad Verbum

Ad verbum — (*word for word*). The school girl crammed the poem ad verbum.

Advise

Advice — (*inform*). I have advised him telegraphically that I am leaving by Deluxe train.

Affair

Affair of honour — (*question one's self-respect*). In the China war, the Indian soldiers were in an affair of honour.

Affiliate

Affiliate with — (*attached with*). P.N. College is affiliated with Delhi University

Affiliate to — (*to be a member of*). I am affiliated to the Congress Party.

Affront

To affront — (*to insult*). Mohan offered an affront to his father.

Afield

Far afield — (*at a distance*). The economic regeneration of Pakistan is still far afield.

After

To look after — (*to take care of*). The women should always look after the house and men should work in offices.

After all — (*everything being taken into account*). After all he is your brother, you must not behave like that.

Hanker after — (*to go about desperately*). An intelligent person should not hanker after a clerical job.

Look before and after — (*to think*). A wise man always looks before and after while doing any thing.

Again

Now and again — (*occasionally*). I visit Kanpur now and again.

As much again — (*twice as much : double*). I cannot sell this book for two rupees : even if you pay me as much again, it will still be below my cost price.

Time and again; Over and over again; Again and again — (*often; repeatedly*). The teacher explained the problem again and again till every student understood it.

Against

Against a rainy day — (*in preparation for hard days*). It is wise to keep some money against a rainy day.

To work against time — (*to work with a view to finishing it within a given time*). We are asking all the labourers of our factory to work against time for completing the Government contract before the end of this month.

To run against — (*to meet by chance*). I ran against Suneeta in Mumbai during my last visit.

Age

A golden age — (*a prosperous period*). Years 1982 and 1983 were a golden age for my brother's business.

To come of age — (*to become major; to attain the age of 21*). Surekha got married when she came of age.

For ages — (*for a long time*). My brother has not written me for ages.

Agency

By the agency of — (*through the help of*). By the agency of God, we completed our Himalayan expedition.

Ago

Long, long ago — (*many, many years back*). Long, long ago, there was a king named Bharat who sacrificed everything for the well-being of his nation.

Agree

Agree with — (*to consent*). I fully agree with you.

Agree to — (*to concur*). The whole family agreed to the suggestion of Naresh.

Agree on — (*approve*). At last the family agreed on to carry on the business jointly.

Agog

To be all agog — (*to be eager*). The whole nation was all agog to have the last glimpse of Pandit Nehru.

Ahead

To go ahead — (*to advance*). Go ahead with your plans.

Aim

Aim at — (*to make up the mind for a definite purpose*). He aims at becoming a pilot one day.

Air

On the air — (*broadcasting by wireless*). The morning news is now on the air.

To take air — (*to become known*). The secrets of the Chinese Government soon took air.

In the air — (*undecided*). Many Indian plans remain in the air.

To give a person the air — (*to dismiss him*). A dishonest person is given the air in no time.

Air-worthy — (*fit to be flown*). This helicopter is air worthy.

An air-absurdity — (*an appearance of foolishness*). He is always having an air of absurdity.

Airy — (*light hearted*). Many women are airy hence cannot be depended upon.

Ajar

To be ajar — (*half open*). When we reach home, we found the door ajar.

Alarm

To raise an alarm — (*to give notice of danger*). When the fire broke out in Sadar Bazar, the people of the locality raised an alarm.

To take alarm — (*to be frightended*). A person who always takes alarm cannot prosper in life.

Alive

To look alive — (*to be brisk*). Even at seventy he looks alive.

Alas

Alas the day — (*unhappy day*). Alas the day when Pandit Nehru lost his life.

All

All and sundry — (*individually and collectively*). The law applies to all and sundry.

All over with — (*finished*). It is all over with the previous contract, let us look for a new one now.

All in all — (*complete master*). The manager is all in all in offering you this post.

All one — (*just the same*). It is all one for him wheather his son passes the examination this time or not.

All-out — (*involving one's all strength or resources*). I made an all-out attempt to get through the examination.

All-rounder — (*able in various walks of life*). He is an all-rounder, well up both in studies and in games.

For good and all — (*finally*). I have settled my accounts with my office people for good and all.

All through — (*every part*). The mechanic has looked all through his scooter.

All of a sudden — (*suddenly*)

Allot

Allot — (*assign*). This house is allotted to me.

Allow

Allow for — (*to take into consideration*). While marking the papers, an examiner always allows for cleanliness.

Allowance

To make allowance for — (*to take into consideration*). In offering this job, we should make allowance for family background.

Along

All along — (*constantly*). All along you had been saying that you want to go to Calcutta and now when the opportunity has arisen, you decline to do so.

Along with — (*in the company of*). Next time when I go abroad I shall take my wife along with me.

Aloof

To keep aloof — (*to remain at a distance*). Students should always keep aloof from politics.

Altar

To lead to the alter — (*to marry*). Krishna led Gautam to the altar.

Amend

To make amends — (*to compensate*). The teacher advised Sohan to make amends for his conduct.

Amiss

To take amiss — (*misunderstand*). You may tell me whatever you want, I will not take amiss.

Not amiss — (*nothing wrong about it*). To reprimand an erring child sometimes is not amiss.

Amuck

To run amuck — (*to run about madly murdering people indiscriminately*). At the time of partition of our country many persons ran amuck.

Anchor

At anchor — (*standing still*). We boarded the ship when it was at anchor.

To come to anchor — (*to halt the ship*). After fifteen hour's sailing the ship came to anchor.

Ancient

The Ancient of Days — (*God*). A man who trusts in the ancient of days, generally succeeds in life.

Angel

Angel of death — (*messenger of death*). Cholera is the angel of death.

Visits like angels — (*rate visits*). Now-a-days your visits are like angels.

Animal

Animal spirits — (*cheerful and full of life*). This young boy is full of animal spirits.

Anon

Ever and anon — (*every now and then*). He comes to my place ever and anon.

Answer

Answer — (*correspond to*). This answers to my question.

To answer — (*succeed*). I am afraid his efforts will not answer.

To answer back answer — (*to rebuke saucily*). In any case his mother should not have answered back the answer.

Antidote

To act as antidote — (*to neutralize*). Truth acts as an antidote to falsehood.

Any

At any rate — (*whatever may happen*). At any rate, I must get first class in the examination.

Anyone — (*anybody*). The question is so simple that anyone can solve it.

Apart

To set apart — (*to devote*). Some time must be set apart for daily prayers.

Ape

God's ape — (*a born fool*). He is a God's ape.

Apex

On the apex — (*culminating point*). During his last years of life Jawahar Lal Nehru stood on the apex.

Apostle

Apostle of peace — (*one who preaches peace*). Mahatma Gandhi was an apostle of peace.

Apostle of — (*advocate of*). He is an apostle of truth.

Appeal

Appeal — (*influencing power*). Beauty has its own appeal.

To appeal — (*fascinate*). A beautiful girl always appeals to the eyes.

Appearance

To all appearances — (*so far as can be seen*). Thomson is an honest person to all appearances.

To put in an appearance — (*to show oneself*). Only in a few important public functions, the Prime Minister puts in an appearance.

To keep up appearances — (*to maintain an outward show*). Punjabi families generally try to keep up appearances.

Apple

Apple of discord — (*cause of quarrel*). Property is an apple of discord among brothers.

Apple of the eye — (*something especially dear*). Rahim is the apple of his father's eye.

To upset the apple-cart — (*to spoil one's plans*). His bad habits have upset the apple-cart of his life's ambitions.

Apply

Apply for — He has applied for a clerical post.

To apply oneself to — (*to devote*). The teacher advised the students to apply themselves to studies.

Appointment

To fix up appointment — (*to fix up an engagement with a person at a particular time*). Please fix an appointment with the manager before you can see him.

To keep an appointment — (*to appear on time at the fixed place*). He always keeps his appointment.

Architect

To be the architect of — (*maker*). A truly great man is the architect of his destiny.

Argue

To argue one out of — (*to satisfy by reasoning against*). One cannot argue a drunkard out of his cup.

To argue into — (*to persuade towards a course of action*). Whatever arguments you may give him, he is not going to be argued into your sentiments.

To argue it away (*to get rid of by reasoning*). Unemployment in the country cannot be argued away.

Arm

Arm in arm — (*interlinked*). Gandhi and Nehru walked arm in arm.

To bear arms — (*carry arms*). During the national emergency, every Indian should know how to bear arms.

It arms — (*armed*). Africa is in arms against colonialism.

Under arms — (*in the army*). During the peace period the number of soldiers under arms is reduced to the minimum.

To lay down arms — (*to cease hostilities*). The Indo-Pakistan armies have to laid down arms.

Up in arms — (*actively engaged in rebellion*). The Hindus were up in arms against Muslims during the partition.

King of arms — (*chief herald*). Indira Gandhi was the king of arms in politics.

Art

Art and part — (*design and execution*). We have no art and part in Vimla's affairs.

Black art — (*magic*). Gogia Pasha earns his living through black art.

Ashes

Sackcloth and ashes — (*symbol of repentance*). The defeated nations do not wear sackcloth and ashes.

To lay in ashes — (*to burn to the ground*). The whole factory lay in ashes.

To bring back the ashes — (*to wipe out defeat*). English cricketers did their best to bring back the ashes from Australia.

At

At the bottom of — (*the source of*). Terrorists were at the bottom of the conspiracy against the President.

At daggers drawn — (*extremely bitter enmity*). Satish and Vinay are at daggers drawn now-a-days.

At home in — (*fully acquainted*). He is at home at English.

At large — (*unrestrained*). The thief was at large when the police made vain efforts to catch him.

At the top of — (*with maximum force*). He shouted at the top of his voice.

At a loss — (*to be puzzled*). I am at a loss to understand what made you go to David's house.

At liberty — (*free to do anything*). He is at liberty to do anything these days.

At a standstill — (*without any further movement*). The talks of professors of G.K. College are again at a standstill.

At fault — (*in the wrong*). When you say you are not familiar with the problem, you are at fault.

Attendance

To dance attendance — (*to attend to the convenience of*). Clerks dance attendance on the Superintendent.

Avail

To avail oneself of — (*to have it or to benefit therefrom*). I will avail myself of this golden chance.

Away

To do away with — (*to make an end of anything*). He will have to do away with his lazy habits or else he will never prosper.

To make away with — (*to kill*). The thief made away with all the members of the family.

Awry

To go awry — (*to go astray*). Many a young men goes awry.

Axe

Axe to grind — (*to serve a private purpose*). I do not like Suraj, he is always in the habit of grinding his own axe.

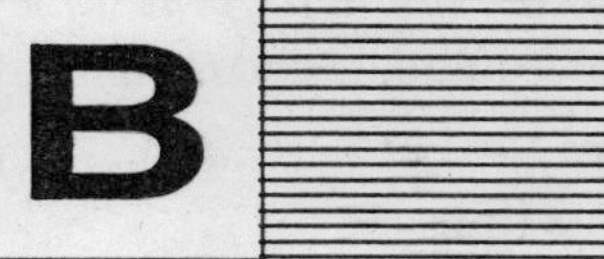

Baby

To hold the baby — (*to take over temporarily a thankless job*). While the manager controls the office, an assistant merely holds the baby.

Back

Behind one's back — (*during one's absence*). Behind my back at the office, my assistant puts everything in disorder.

To back up — (*to support*). For a good cause one must always back up.

To turn one's back upon — (*to turn away*). It is shame on you to turn your back upon your friends in trouble.

Back and belly — (*clothing and food*). It is very hard to earn back and belly now-a-days.

Backstair influence — (*secret and illegitimate influence*). Come what may, I will get a job without backstair influence.

Back and forth — (*to and fro*). She was walking back and forth in the corridor.

To set one's back — (*to make one angry*). I don't think it is advisable to set anybody's backup.

To the backbone — (*thoroughly*). Rajiv is honest to the backbone.

Bacon

To save one's bacon — (*to save one's baby*). During partition everyone tried to save his bacon.

To bring him to bacon — (*to succeed in one's purpose*). I had to work before I brought home the bacon.

Bad

Bad blood — (*ill feeling*). Do not have bad blood with anyone.

Bad time — (*unfavourable time*). During the bad time only a few relatives and friends stand by.

Bad form — (*ill manners*). A person with bad form does not succeed in life.

Bag

Bag and baggage — (*with all belongings*). He left India with bag and baggage.

Bag of bones — (*a lean creature*). Manmohan is a mere bag of bones.

In the bottom of the bag — (*as a last resort*). He had his gun in the bottom of his bag to help his brother in the fight.

Balance

Balanced personality — (*a steady mind*). Mahatma Gandhi had a balanced personality.

To lose one's balance — (*to fall physically*). White getting down from the car my wife lost balance.

Balance of advantage — (*great influence*). He has balance of advantage in getting the job of an overseer.

Ball

To keep the ball rolling — (*to do one's part in a talk*). Try to keep your ball rolling while on picnics and parties.

To have the ball to one's feet — (*to see one's way to success*). After very hard labour I was at last able to have the ball to my feet.

Bank

To bank upon — to (*depend*). Even at the age of thirty he banks upon his parents.

Baptism

Baptism on fire — (*soldier's first battle*). Balbir Singh has had baptism of fire in NEFA.

Baptism of blood — (*martyrdom*). Maharani of Jhansi accepted the baptism of blood at the alter of the freedom of India.

Bargain

Dutch bargain — (*a bargain ending with drink*). In all bargains, the drunkards always prefer the Dutch bargains.

Into the bargain — (*over and above*). After buying the sofa set we went into the bargain of a foreign dressing table.

To strike a bargain — (*to come to terms*). The British struck a bargain with the Congress for the Independence of India.

Bark

Bark worse than bite — (*of testy harmless persons*). The school teacher's bark is always worse than his bite.

Bat

Off one's own bat — (*by one's own efforts*). I have made all money entirely off my own bat.

Battery

To turn a man's battery against himself — (*to defeat a person with his own arguments*). I turned his battery against himself while discussing politics with him.

Bay

To stand at bay — (*to show fight*). At last they agreed to stand at bay to remove their misunderstanding.

To bay at the moon — (*thinking of something impossible to be achieved*). Your efforts are all baying at the moon.

Be

Be-all and end-all — (*the final result*). One should never be too proud as death is the be-all and end-all of all human beings.

Bear

To bear down — (*to defeat*). Pandit Nehru always bore down his opposition.

To bear out — (*to confirm*). I bore out his statement.

To bear with — (*to tolerate*). I cannot bear with a statement like that of yours.

To bear a hand — (*to help*). Please bear me a hand in placing this trunk on my head.

Beat

To beat about the bush — (*to approach a subject in a roundabout way*). Please do not beat about the bush and come to the point.

To beat the air — (*to strive in vain*). We did not beat the air for the freedom of our country.

To beat off — (*to drive back by force*). It is difficult to beat off Americans in any battle.

To beat upon — (*to strike upon again and again*). When an earthquake beats upon houses start falling down.

Beauty

Beauty sleep — (*sleep before midnight*). It is unwise to disturb a man while in beauty sleep.

Beauty Queen — (*the most beautiful lady in the region*). Suneeta is the beauty queen of I.P. College.

Become

To become of — (*to happen; the end of*). What will become of his sons after his death ?

Bed

A bed of roses — (*a condition of comfort or luxury*). Life is not a bed of roses.

To take to bed — (*to get sick*). He has been taken to bed for the last ten days.

Bed fellow — (*a close friend*). Krishan and Mohan are bed fellows.

Before

Beforehand — (*before time*). The Frontier Mail arrived beforehand yesterday.

Before long — (*soon*). You don't worry, everything will go well before long.

Beg

To beg the question — (*to assume truth of the matter of dispute*). To say the man is a human being is like begging the question.

Beggar

To beggar description — (*beyond one's power to describe*). The beauty of Kashmir beggars description.

Begin

To begin with — (*in the first place*). To begin with I am not acquainted with Indian history.

To begin the world — (*to start in life*). It is very difficult to begin the world now-a-days.

Behind

Behind the scenes — (*in private*). The principal and the lecturers are having their discussions behind the scenes.

Behind the time — (*late*). The main reason for the dismissal from service was his being behind the time.

Fall behind — (*not keep up with*). He has fallen behind in English studies.

Behind one's back — (*in somebody's absence*). I do not like your habit of criticising a man behind his back.

Bell

To bell the cat — (*a take the lead in a dangerous work*). Who will bell the cat ?

To sound clear as bell — (*to sound quite clear*). His love for you sounds clear as a bell.

Below

Below one's breath — (*silently*). We are talking below our breath.

Below the mark — (*not up to the standard*). His work is below the mark.

Bench

To be raised to the bench — (*to become a judge*). Ram Mohan has been raised to the bench.

Bend

Bend one's knee — (*to be humble before*). Never bend your knees before anybody except God.

Beneath

Beneath contempt — (*not worthy of contempt*). The Prime Minister thought him beneath contempt.

Benefit

Benefit of doubt — (*assuming doubt rather than guilt*). The court gave him the benefit of doubt.

Beside

Beside the mark — (*irrelevant*). I don't like your talking beside the mark, please come to the point.

Best

To make the best of things — (*be contented*). The sure way to happiness is to make the best of things available.

At best — (*at the most*). At best I can offer you a salary of Rs. 600/- per month.

To the best of my belief — (*so far as I know*). To the best of my belief, he is a reasonable man.

Better

To get the better of — (*to defeat*). A weak man cannot get the better of a strong man.

Better late than never — (*something which is necessary should be done even after some delay*). Even if you start with your studies now it will be better late than never.

Better off — (*to be in a superior position*). He is definitely better off as compared to his friend.

One's betters — (*one's superiors*). One should always respect one's betters.

Between

Between two fires — (*to earn displeasure of both the parties*). A wise arbitrator always avoids to be between two fires.

Between the cup and the lip — (*between hope and reality*). There is many a slip between the cup and the lip.

Between the devil and the deep sea — (*in difficulties from both sides*). Please do not trouble me any more. I am always between the devil and the deep sea.

Beyond

Beyond measure — (*unmeasurable*). The success achieved by Vimal is beyond measure.

To go beyond — (*to surpass*). Never go beyond reality.

Bid

Bid good-bye — (*to take leave of the departing person*). As soon the train whistled he bade good-bye to his friend.

To bid welcome — (*to receive cordially*). We were ready to bid welcome to the marriage party.

Big

To talk big — (*to talk pompously*). He is in the habit of talking big.

To look big — (*to impress one's prosperity*). Reality is reality, looking big will not convince me.

Big with young — (*pregnant*). She is big with a young now-a-days.

Bind

Bind over — (*to place legal restriction upon).* The country has been bound over to keep the peace for two years.

Bird

A bird's eye view — (*a general view*). We could hardly have a bird's eye view at the time of Panditji's cremation.

Bird of same feather — (*persons of similar habits*). Birds of the same feather flock together.

Bird in hand — (*certainty*). A bird in hand is worth two in the bush.

To kill two birds with one stone — (*to gain two ends with one attempt*). Politicians normally kill two birds with one stone.

Bit

Bit by bit — (*gradually*). I don't mind if you do it bit by bit, but do it well.

To take the bit in the teeth — (*to be beyond control*). This work is to take the bit in the teeth for you.

Bit and sup — (*something to eat and drink*). Please give me bit and sup, I am very hungry.

To give a bit of one's mind — (*to speak frankly*). When I asked him for some money, he gave a bit of his mind and said no.

Black

Black and white — (*in writing*). Please give me everything in black and white that you have said now.

A black sheep — (*one having a bad reputation*). There are some black sheep in our college.

Blackmail — (*extracting money by threats*). You can no longer blackmail him as full details have already been published in the papers.

Blackhole — (*military lock-up*). During every war many soldiers are blackholed by opposite groups.

Blind

Blind man's holiday — (*time before lighting a candle*). Rashmi and Papu enjoy blind man's holiday.

Blindfold — (*reckless*). Your blindfold habits will ruin you one day.

Block

Block up — (*to obstruct*). Land slides have blocked up the Srinagar road.

Chip of the old block — (*just like the father*). His child is chip of the old block.

Blood

Flesh and blood — (*human beings*). A flesh and blood is never happy in life.

In cold blood — (*deliberately*). He killed his wife in cold blood.

In hot blood — (*under excitement*). He killed his wife in hot blood.

Blood and iron — (*relentless use of force*). Hitler mastered Germany through blood and iron.

Blow

To blow up — (*to shatter*). His plans were all blown up.

To blow one's own trumpet — (*to praise oneself*). One cannot succeed by blowing one's own trumpet.

To come to blows — (*to come to fight*). After their heated discussion both the groups came to blows.

Blow over — (*to pass away*). The rain has blown over.

Blue

Once in a blue moon — (*rarely; very seldom*). He comes to see me once in a blue moon.

Blunt

To blunt the edge of — (*to weaken force*). Time blunts the edge of anger.

Board

To sweep the board — (*to be all successful*). Jatindra has always been sweeping the board in his life.

Boat

To sail in the same boat — (*having the same fate*). Both husband and wife sail in the same boat.

To have an oar in another's boat — (*interfering in another's affairs*). It is unwise to have an oar in another's boat.

Body

Body and soul — (*wholly; completely*). He devoted his body and soul for getting first class in the B.A. examination.

Bolt

Bolt from the blue — (*complete surprise*). China's attack on NEFA was a bolt from the blue.

Bone

Bone of contention — (*cause of dispute*). Money was the bone of contention between the two brothers.

To pick a bone with someone — (*to dispute*). I do not want to pick a bone with anyone.

To the bone — (*to the inmost part*). He is a speaker to the bone.

Book

To be in one's good books — (*to be one's favourite*). He is in the good books of the manager.

To bring to book — (*to be in disfavour*). He is dead; it is no use bringing him to book.

To be in one's bad books — (*commanding a bad opinion*). He is in the bad books of his manager.

Boot

To make boot of — (*to profit*). The new policy of the Government is going to punish those who are making boots by charging higher prices.

To be given the boot — (*to be dismissed*). He has been given the boot from the service.

Born

To be born with a silver spoon in one's mouth — (*to be a rich man's child*), Sumedha was born with a silver spoon in her mouth.

To be born under a luck star — (*to be lucky by birth*). He is born under a lucky star.

Bosom

Bosom friend — (*fast friend*). Mohan and Sohan are bosom friends.

Bottle

Over the bottle — (*while drinking*). Let's discuss the matter over the bottle.

Bottom

From the bottom of the heart — (*sincerely*). I love you from the bottom of my heart.

To be at the bottom of — (*to be the real cause of*). Who is at the bottom of this dispute ?

Bound

By leaps and bounds — (*most rapidly*). If we walk at this speed we shall reach there by leaps and bounds.

Out of bounds — (*not within limits for movement*). Soldiers are out of bounds after 10 p.m. in many civil areas.

Bow

To draw the long bow — (*to make long statements*). Our principal is in the habit of drawing the long bow.

Bowing acquaintance — (*a slight acquaintance*). Although I have a bowing acquaintance with him, I feel I shall be able to convince him to offer you a suitable job.

To have two strings in one's bow — (*to have more than one resource*). An intelligent person has always two strings in his bow.

Box

To be in the box — (*to be in a fix*). He is in the box now-a-days.

Brain

To blow out one's brains — (*to shoot to kill*). During the war soldiers are ordered to blow out one's brain.

Bread

Bread and butter — (*livelihood*). For an average man it is very hard to earn bread and butter these days.

Butter on both sides — (*easy prosperity*). The Dalmia family enjoys butter on both sides.

Know which side one's bread is buttered — (*to know one's interests*). A wise man knows which side his bread is buttered.

Break

To break into — (*to enter forcibly*). The thief broke into the house and escaped with the money.

To break off — (*to appear suddenly*). My brother broke off when we were taking lunch.

To break with — (*to cease to be on friendly terms*). I have broken with Ramesh.

To break down — (*to fail*). After running just a few miles the car broke down.

To break up — (*to disperse*). The tear-gas broke up the crowd.

To break through — (*to overcome*). He has broken through all difficulties.

Breast

To make a clean breast of — (*confess*). Sussie went to the church to make a clean breast of her sins.

Breathe

To breathe one's last — (*to die*). Pandit Nehru breathed his last on 27th May 1964.

Brief

In brief — (*in short*). Please describe the matter in brief.

Bring

To bring about — (*to cause to happen*). His negligence brought about his failure.

Bring up — (*to educate and train*). That orphan child was brought up by Krishna's parents.

To bring out — (*to produce*). We are thinking of bringing out a book on idioms.

To bring down — (*to humble*). Please bring down your anger and then talk.

To bring in — (*to yield*). Our factory is bringing in ten maunds of flour daily.

To bring to mind — (*to recall*). Please bring to mind, I paid you rupees ten last Sunday.

To bring to light — (*to make known*). The Das Commission has brought to light the evils of the Punjab Chief Minister.

Broken

Broken-hearted — (*crushed in grief*). Having lost his wife, he fell broken-hearted.

Brush

Brush up — (*to renew*). Let us brush up our acquaintances.

Brush away — (*to put aside*). Unless he can brush away his weaknesses, he cannot change himself.

Bubble

To prick the bubble — (*to destroy an illusion*). Defeat and death prick the bubble of life.

Bucket

To kick the bucket — (*to die*). The end of every human being is to kick the bucket one day.

To give the bucket — (*to dismiss*). I have given the bucket to my clerk today.

Bud

To nip in the bud — (*to kill in the very beginning*). Nip the evil in the bud.

Build

To build castles in the air — (*to plan visionary and impossible scheme*). It is no use building castles in the air; do something solid.

Bull

Tc take the bull by the horns — (*to face a danger with courage*). Soldiers always take the bull by the horns.

Burn

To burn the candle at both ends — (*to waste money or health quickly*). A teacher's duty is to advise the students not to burn the candle at both ends.

To burn one's fingers — (*to suffer from interfering in others' affairs*). Confine to your work and do not burn your fingers by muddling in others affairs.

Burn daylight — (*to waste time*). I don't like people burning daylight.

Burst

To burst into tears — (*to fall crying*). On seeing her injured husband she burst into tears.

By

By and by — (*slowly*). Do things by and by but do them well.

By the by — (*incidently*). By the by, were you in Mumbai last month ?

By dint of — (*by virtue of*). By dint of hard work, he secured first position in the University.

Cake

A piece of cake — (*something easy and pleasant*). Life these days is not a piece of cake.

Call

To call up — (*to recollect*). It is difficult for me to call up the whole happening as I fainted afterwards.

To call on — (*to pay a brief visit*). Please call on us this evening.

To call bad names — (*to abuse*). It is no good to call him bad names.

To call away — (*to divert*). His attention was called away by the appearance of a young girl.

To call for — (*to require*). His way of working will can for his explanation.

To call into being — (*to create*). God has called the whole world into being.

To call attention to — (*to point*). He was called attention to his mischiefs.

Candle

Not fit to hold a candle — (*not to be compared with*). Pakistan is not fit to hold a candle against India.

To burn the candle at both ends — (*to waste money or health*). A wise man never burns the candle at both ends.

Candle power — (*unit for the measurement of light*). This is a 20-candle power lamp.

Cap

A feather in one's cap — (*something to be proud of*). Getting first position in the university is really a feather in one's cap.

Cap in hand — (*humbly*). The foreign ambassador stood before the President with his cap in his hand.

Capital

Capital error — (*blunder*). By giving employment to that fellow you have made a capital error.

A capital sentence — (*death as punishment*). At last the court decided to give a capital sentence to Ghanshyam for the murder of his wife.

Card

House of cards — (*a weak scheme*). If you work on a house of cards, you will never be successful.

To have one's cards on the table — (*to have no secret*). Having one's cards on the table always is not wise sometimes.

Throw up the cards — (*to accept defeat*). You have no way out now except to throw up your cards.

To speak by the cards — (*to speak to the point and to speak well*). Sardar Patel always spoke by the cards.

Care

To take care of — (*to look after*). After the death of his father he has now to take care of his mother.

Carpet

On the carpet — (*under discussion*). Election of the Assembly for Punjab is still on the carpet.

Carry

To carry out — (*to execute*). During five years of my service with IAC, I carried out my duties properly.

To carry on — (*to manage*). It is very difficult to carry on with a family of five members with Rs. 200 per month.

To carry off — (*to be killed*). He was carried off in storm.

To carry the day — (*to win*). Let us see who carries the day in the last Test match.

Cart

To put the cart before the horse — (*to reverse the natural order*). If you think of getting first division without doing hard labour, you are putting the cart before the horse.

Case

In any case — (*in all events*). In any case we must reach there before 4 p.m.

Cash

Hard cash — (*ready money*). How much hard cash do you have ?

Out of cash — (*without any money*). I am out of cash these days.

Cast

Cast down — (*to depress*). Do not cast down your child with fears, let him study further.

To cast a glance at — (*to see*). During Durga Pooja people go to cast a glance at the Goddess.

Cast away — (*to waste*). I cannot afford to cast away any more money.

The last cast — (*the last venture*). This is the last cast of Sohan in 10th class. He is not going to try next year.

Cast up — (*give up*). I don't want to cast up the scheme, it took two months in planning.

Cat

Cat and dog life — (*full of quarrels*). All these four years I had been living a cat and dog life with my wife.

To let the cat out of the bag — (*to reveal a secret*). Women generally let the cat out of the bag.

Cat's paw — (*tool of another person*). One cannot be successful for long working on cat's paw.

Catch

To catch a Tartar — (*to fight with a stranger enemy*). In Vietnam the Americans have caught a Tartar.

To catch sight of — (*to suddenly get glimpses of*). While in the train we caught sight of a river.

To catch one's breath — (*to check suddenly*). When the candidate was copying, the examiner caught his breath.

Cause

First cause — (*the original cause*). God alone is the first cause of life.

Cave

To cave in — (*to acknowledge defeat*). The manager caved in before the director's arguments.

Chalk

To chalk out — (*to plan*). Let us chalk out our programme of studies.

Change

To change colours — (*to turn pale*). When I saw her in the company of Boota Singh, she started changing her colours.

To get no change out of — (*fail to defeat one*). Mohammad could get no change out of Ahmed on account of his being clever.

Check

To keep in check — (*to keep under control*). Keep your children in check.

Chew

To chew the cud — (*to reflect*). Writers always chew the cud.

Chicken

Chicken-hearted — (*a coward*). Dinesh is a chicken hearted fellow.

Child

Child's play — (*an easy thing to do*). Climbing the Himalayas is not a child's play.

Child wife — (*very young wife*). Gandhiji was married to a child wife.

Chip

Chip of the old block — (*same*). They are chips of the old block.

Chuck

To give one the chuck — (*to dismiss*). The manager gave the peon the chuck.

Choose

Pick and choose — (*to select with care*). In the pick and choose of books at the shop he lost his purse.

Clap

Clap on the back — (*encouragement*). When John passed his matric examination, his father clapped him on the back.

To clap hand — (*to make an agreement*). All the members of the party finally clapped their hands.

Clay

Clay-brained — (*stupid*). Our teacher is clay-brained, he is always on the look out of beating boys.

Clean

Clean slate — (*a fresh start*). Unless both of you have a clean slate, you cannot come to any agreement.

Clean-handedness — (*innocence*). Although I know everything, yet I showed clean-handedness in the whole affair.

To make a clean breast of — (*to admit frankly*). I am ready to make a clean breast of my mistakes.

Clear

Clear the way — (*to make the way open*). These steps will clear the way for our future programme.

Clock

Like clockwork — (*regularly*). He takes his exercise like clockwork.

Cloth

To cut one's coat according to cloth — (*to adjust expenditure according to income*). Wise is one who cuts his coat according to his cloth.

Cloud

In the clouds — (*in the world of imagination*). He lost his career in the clouds.

Cloud on brow — (*depressed look*). He could not easily see a cloud on Ravinder's brow.

Under a cloud — (*in disfavour*). He could not get any promotion because he was always under the cloud of his manager.

Cloud-castle — (*day dream*). Vimla passes her time in cloud-castles.

Coal

To carry coal to Newcastle — (*to do superfluous work*). Many young persons are in the habit of carrying coal to Newcastle now-a-days.

Coat

Turn coat — (*one who changes his principles*). A person in the habit of turning coat never succeeds in life.

Cock

A cock and bull story — (an *unbelievable story*). We are not going to work on your cock and bull story.

To live like a fighting cock — (*to live on the best food*). The rich family lives like a fighting cock now-a-days.

That cock won't fight — (*that scheme will not work*). That cock of yours will not fight.

Cold

To have cold feet — (*not to fight*). The General had cold feet in the last war.

In cold blood — (*deliberately*). He murdered his whole family in cold blood.

Cold comfort — (*uninteresting*). The whole party was a cold comfort.

Column

Fifth columnist — (*one who works against the interests of his own country*). There are many fifth columnists in every country of the world.

Come

To come to blows — (*to fight*). After their heated discussion, leaders of both the groups came to blows.

To come across — (*to meet with*). While going to bazaar, I came across a big snake this morning.

To come out — (*to appear*). Suddenly during the interval, all the actors of the film came out on the stage.

To come to light — (*to reveal*). Many things have come to light now.

To come down with — (*to pay money*). Wait, I will come down with ten rupees.

To come by — (*to gain*). How did you come by rupees five hundred ?

To come up to — (*to reach*). The train has come up to the outer signal).

To come round — (*to recover*). The patient will soon come round.

To come to a standstill — (*to come to stop*). The train has come to a standstill.

Company

To keep company — (*to go together*). They always keep company.

Conscience

In all conscience — (*certainly*). In all conscience I will get first class in the examination.

Consent

Age of consent — (*age at which a girl can be married without consulting her parents*). Purnima has reached the age of consent.

Contact

To be in contact with — (*to be in touch with*). We were in contact with Mohan so long we were at Mumbai.

Contempt

To hold in contempt — (*to hate*). He is held in contempt by his colleagues.

Contempt of court — (*interference with the administration of justice*). The Minister of State was found guilty of contempt of court.

Contrary

On the contrary — (*otherwise*). You should be ashamed of beating that little child; on the contrary you feel happy in that.

Corn

To tread on one's corns — (*to injure one's feelings*). One should not tread on one's corns.

Corner

To turn the corner — (*to escape the crisis*). Now the family has been able to turn the corner.

To cut off the corner — (*to take a short-cut*). By cutting off a corner, we reached Connaught Place in fifteen minutes.

To put in the corner — (*to punish*). The child was put in the corner by his father.

All the corners of the earth — (*everywhere*). We have searched all the corners of the earth but we have not been able to find Sudesh anywhere.

To drive one into the corner — (*to put in a fix*). Do not depend on Mohan; he will always drive you into the corner.

Cost

At the cost of — (*at the expense of*). You cannot succeed at the cost of others.

To count the cost — (*to consider the risk*). Please count the cost of working on his plan.

Count

To count upon — (*to depend*). How long can one count upon one's parents ?

Crack

In a crack — (*in a moment*). I shall be there in a crack.

Crop

To crop up — (*happen unexpectedly*). Since he has declined to study further, the problem of finding a job for him has cropped up now.

Cross

To cross the path of — (*to stand in one's way*). Please do not cross the path of my work.

Crow

As the crow flies — (*in a straight line*). The children are always advised to go as the crow flies to their homes after the close of their school.

Cry

A far cry — (*a great distance*). Mumbai is a far cry from Delhi.

To cry down — (*to condemn*). The Punjab politics is being cried down now-a-days.

To cry against — (*to protest against*). Let us cry against the bad behaviour of our employers.

Cup

There are many a slip between the cup and the lip — (*The possibility of something unfortunate happening at the last moment*).

Cup was full — (*was complete*). After the death of the Prime Minister, the cup of the nation was full of misery.

Curry

To curry favour — (*flatter*). Clerks generally try to curry favour with their officers.

Curtain

Behind the curtain — (*away from public gaze*). Many policies of the Government are discussed behind the curtain.

Cut

Short cut — (*one which shortens the distance*). Let us take a short cut to Connaught Place.

To cut the coat according to the cloth — (*to adjust expenditure according to financial circumstances*). A wise man always cuts his coat according to his cloth.

To cut both ways — (*to be equally applicable for and against*). His arguments cut both ways.

To cut down — (*to reduce*). In the interest of the country the Government must cut down its expenditure on defence.

To cut to the heart — (*to wound one's feelings*). By saying that he is a thief, he cut him to the heart.

Damocles

Sword of Damocles — (*a big danger*). The Pakistan-China alliance is a sword of Damocles hanging over India.

Damp

To strike a damp into — (*to discourage*). I don't know why some parents strike a damp into the heart of their children in doing some initiative work.

To damp the enthusiasm — (*to chill*). Your working has damped the enthusiasm of the whole society.

Dance

To dance attendance upon — (*to flatter*). A subordinate always tries to dance attendance upon his superiors.

Dark

To be in the dark about — (*possessing no knowledge*). Do not pose to be in the dark about the matter.

A leap in the dark — (*unknown danger*). China's attack on India was a leap in the dark.

The dark ages — (*earlier periods of history*). During the dark ages, a man had very limited wants.

Prince of darkness — (*the devil*). May the prince of darkness plague the wicked.

Dash

To dash one's hopes — (*to make one completely hopeless*). Your own action is responsible for dashing your hopes.

Dash of good blood — (*of noble qualities*). Manmohan does not have a dash of good blood in him.

To cut a dash — (*to make a brilliant show*). Gogia Pasha cut a dash in his last performance in Delhi.

Date

Have a date — (*appointment*). I have a date with him hence can't come to your place.

Out-of-date — (*old fashioned*). Chooridar pyjama is out-of-date.

Up-to-date — (*latest*). My accounts are always up-to-date these days.

Day

Day of doom — (*Judgement Day*). A thief should never forget the day of doom.

To lose the day — (*to lose war*). At last China lost its day to India.

Every dog has his day — (*No one is always unlucky*).

D-Day — (*Dooms Day*). July 4th is a D-Day for the English in America.

Dead

Dead drunk — (*completely drunk*). He came dead drunk late at night.

Dead loss — (*a complete loss*). The books soiled in rain are a dead loss to a bookseller.

At dead of night — (*at midnight*). The thieves stole away the whole cash at dead of night.

A dead-letter — (*a law which is no longer in operation*). Why do you rely on what is a dead-letter now.

Dead stock — (*unsaleable stock*). Unsaleable stock of text books have become deal stock.

Deaf

To be deaf to — (*to be indifferent*). He is a deaf to my suggestions.

Deaf-nut — (*a nut without a kernel*). I can assure you, the business you have started is going to be a deaf-nut.

To give a deaf ear to — (*to disregard*). He gave a deaf ear to the Professor's good advise.

Deal

A good deal — (*a lot*). There is a good deal of fun in it.

Deal in — (*trade in*). He deals in cloth.

Deal out — (*to distribute*). Please deal out the cards properly.

Death

At death's door — (*about to die*). He was at death's door last Sunday.

To be sick unto death — (*tired*). I am quite sick unto death for any more service.

Debt

To be over head and ears in debt — (*to be completely in debt*). He is in debt over head and ears now-a-days.

Defect

To have the defects of one's qualities — (*defects that accompany qualities*). Everybody has the defects of his qualities.

Defence

In defence of — (*in support of*). We are in defence of Johul to select him as our leader.

The best defence is offence — (*one who strikes first achieves superior position*). In war the best defence is offence.

Degree

By degrees — (*gradually*). It pays to do things by degrees.

Third degree methods — (*inhuman torture of the accused*). The police often have to adopt third degree methods to make the culprits confess.

Demarcation

Line of demarcation — (*boundary*). N.E.F.A. is a line of demarcation between India and Pakistan.

Depart

The departed — (*dead*). May God departed soul rest in peace.

Depth

Out of one's depth — (beyond one's faculties). The assignment given to you is out of your depth.

To descend upon — (*to attack*). Pakistan is on the look out to descend upon India.

Descend

To descend upon — (*to attack*). Pakistan is on the look out to descend upon India.

Devil

The devil of — (*unpleasant person*). He is the devil of director.

Give the devil his due — (*give everybody his right*).

Devil's books — (*cards*). Whenever I go there I always find them busy in devil's books.

The devil among — (*disturbance*). I knew there was the devil among the gathering.

Devoid

To be devoid of reason — (*to be foolish*). Are you devoid of all reason; haven't you any sense ?

Devour

To devour the way — (*to go fast*). The camels devoured the way quickly.

Diamond

Black diamond — (*coal*). Black diamond is available in abundance in America.

Die

Upon the die — (*at stake*). Our soldiers killed many Chinese upon the die of their lives.

To die with one — (*to be finished*). Nazi secrets died with Hitler.

To die hard — (*to die with great struggle*). Old habits die hard.

To die in harness — (*to die while still at work*) Pandit Nehru died in harness.

To die daily — (*to suffer spiritual death*). He dies daily.

Differ

To agree to differ — (*to give up an attempt to convince each other*). Kripalani and Menon agreed to differ.

Difference

Make a difference between — (*to treat differently*). Let us not make a difference between the poor and the rich.

To split the difference — (*to come to a compromise*). They came to split the difference after nearly a year.

Dig

To dig in — (*to cover by digging*). The whole position must be dug in now to avoid further difficulties.

To dig at — (*to remark against*). It does not pay to dig at your elders.

Dilemma

Between the horns of a dilemma — (*in practical difficulty*). many a young men are between the horns of a dilemma on the subject of carrier.

Dint

By dint of — (*through the power of*). Sohan was able to get that job by dint of his uncle's influence.

Dip

Dip into — (*to look into it here and there*). Dip into thoroughly and then start a suitable business.

To dip into the future — (*to think of coming events*). On completing his education career, he has to dip into the future for service.

Dirt

To eat dirt — (*to put up with insult*). An honourable man never eats dirts.

To throw dirt at — (*to abuse*). Do not throw dirt at others.

Discord

Apple of discord — (*cause of quarrel*). Money was the apple of discord among the brothers.

Discretion

Age of discretion — (*time of maturity*). Pramila has reached the age of discretion.

At the discretion of — (*by the wish of*). At the discretion of God they have been blessed with a son.

Disguise

A blessing in disguise — (*a misfortune which produces a good result*). An employer's harsh treatment sometimes proves a blessing in disguise to an employee.

Dish

Dish up — (*serve attractively*). Let us sit together and dish up our idea.

Dismal

The dismals — (*low spirits*). He is in the dismals now-a-days.

Dismiss

Dismiss from one's mind — (*to cease to think about a thing*). When he came to know that his parents will not agree to his marrying Radha, he dismissed her from his mind.

Dispense

Dispense with — His services have been dispensed with from Monday.

Dispute

Beyond dispute — (*certainly*). It is beyond dispute that he is a very good boy.

Dissent

Note of dissent — (*note of disagreement*). Many members of the Congress have given note of dissent on the subject of election of a new Chief Minister for Punjab.

Dissolve

Dissolved in tears — (*weeping copiously*). The boy was dissolved in tears.

Distance

To keep one at a distance — (*to treat with reserve*). I am sure he will keep Mohan at a distance.

Within striking distance — (*near enough to hit each other*). Both the armies are standing within striking distance.

Distinction

Distinction without difference — (*not much difference*). It is hardly a distinction without difference for me whether you stay here in the night or not.

Diversity

Unity in diversity — (*to be connected through some inner link*). Almost all nations have some unity in diversity.

Divine

Divine service — (*public worship*). My father is devoting his major time in devine service.

Divine right of kings — (*right to rule as they like*). The days of divine right of kings have gone.

Dizzy

To make dizzy — (*to bewilder*). Sophia Loren made the whole audience dizzy.

Do

To do away with — (*to get rid of*). I want to do away with this job.

To do in the eye — (*to cheat*). The quality of a thief lies in doing in the eye.

To be done for — (*completely ruined*). When he was done for, his brother helped him to come up again in the life.

To do as Romans do — (*to adjust according to surroundings*). When in Rome do as Romans do.

To do with — (*tolerate*). You will have to do with me because there is no other alternative for you.

Have to do with — (*concerned*). He has nothing to do with this matter.

Do nothing —(*useless*). Mohan is a do-nothing fellow.

Dog

To go to the dogs — (*to be ruined*). Due to the fire in his godown he has gone to the dogs.

Dog of war — (*havoc*). The plague has left the dog of war.

To throw to dogs — (*to sacrifice*) Pandit Nehru threw his whole life to the dogs.

To lead the life of a dog — (*to live miserably*). He is leading the life to the dogs.

Dog cheap — (*very cheap*). Mangoes a dog cheap these days.

Dog in the manager — (*one who prevents another from enjoying what one cannot himself*). The habit of playing dog-in-manager is common among many students.

Dollar

Almighty dollar — (*the power of money*). Almighty dollar rules the world.

Donkey

Donkey's years — (*after a long time*). I have seen you after donkey's years.

Doomsday

Till doomsday — (*for ever*). His habits are not going to change till doomsday.

Door

Out of doors — (*in the open air*). The theatre is going on out of doors.

Next door to — (*near*). He stays next door to me.

At death's door — (*about to die*). He is at the death's door now-a-days.

Double

A double dealer — (*a deceitful person*). He is a double dealer.

Double-edged — (*striking both ways*). I appreciate your double-edged argument.

Double eyed (*deeply strained with guilt*). Raj is double-eyed.

Doubled-minded — (*undecided*). You are always double-minded in selecting your career.

Double-faced — (*false*). I am not going to agree to your doubled-faced argument.

Down

Down in one's luck — (*ill-luck*). He has always been down in his luck right from childhood.

To be down with — (*to be suffering from*). He is down with fever.

To hiss down — (*silence*). I request you to hiss down.

To send down — (*to punish*). The thief has been sent down.

Up and down — (*to and fro*). He is walking up and down.

Down-hearted — (*dispirited*). He is bound to be down hearted after losing a job.

To grind down — (*to bring peace by force*). These days of grinding down have gone.

Down and out — (*completely beaten*). India was completely down and out in this year World Olympics.

Dreamland

Dreamland — (*the end of one's dreams*). Managership in a big hotel is my dreamland.

Drag

To drag in — (*to introduce*). Imperial Tobacco Company is going to drag in a new cigarette in the market, next month.

Drag on — (*to go on as such*). I would advise you to finish the matter as early as you can, there is no use in dragging on the same.

Drag up — (*to rear roughly*). Ram was dragged up somehow.

Draught

So suffer the draught — (*to suffer adverse conditions*). His bad behaviour will make him to suffer the draught one day.

Draw/Drawn

Draw back — (*to withdraw*). When he saw nobody listening to his arguments, he drew back.

Draw up — (*to arrange in order*). Will you please draw up my books in the almirah ?

To be drawn — (*to be attracted*). She was the cause of to be drawn in the whole party.

To draw in — (*to reduce*). Unless you draw in your diet you are not going to slim.

To draw on one's memory — (*to try to remember*). I am drawing on my memory, where we first met.

Long drawn agony — (*great suffering*). Life is a long drawn agony for many.

Drawn on — (*to bring about*). Everybody is trying to draw on wealth.

Drink

To drink off — (*to drink the entire quantity in one gulp*). I drunk off the glass of wine.

On the drink — (*drunk*). In the evening, Dev is always on the drink.

To drink up — (*to finish by drinking*). They drank up the party.

To drink hard — (*to be given to excess drinking*). He has been given to drink hard.

Drive

To drive at — (*aiming at*). They are driving at to kill the lion.

To drive out — (*to expel*). The principal drove out Ramesh from the college on account of his misbehaviour.

To drive to the wall — (*to crush*). It is no bravery in driving the weaker to the wall.

To drive one out of one's senses — (*to madden*). Anger drives one out of his senses.

Drop

To drop a hint — (*to give an indication*). I have dropped a hint that they are going to dismiss you from service.

To drop on one's knees — (*to humble oneself*). One must drop on one's knees before God.

To drop a remark — (*to speak casually*). They are only dropping a remark now-a-days.

To take drop — (*to drink liquor*). let us take a drop.

Drown

Drown out — (*driven out by flood*). The whole village has been drowned out.

Dry

Dry facts — (*uninteresting ideas*). Please do not bore me with your dry facts.

To go dry —(*to be without liquor*). Many cities have gone dry in India now-a-days.

Dry as dust — (*dull*). The picture was absolutely dry as dust.

Dry beat — (*a good beat but not resulting into shedding of blood*). The thief was given a dry beat.

Duck

Duck diamond — (*beloved*). I can give up everything for my duck diamond.

To play ducks and drakes — (*squander*). Malhotra has played ducks and drakes with his wealth.

Dull

Dull brained — (*stupid fellow*). Do not talk to him, he is a dull-brained person.

Dust

To throw dust in one's eyes — (*to deceive*). Try your best, you cannot throw dust in my eyes.

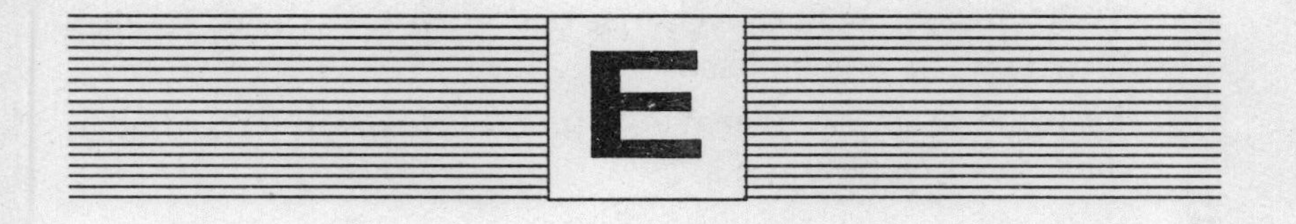

Eagle

Eagle-eyed — (*keen-sighted*). Nothing can remain secret before the eagle-eyed Income-tax Officer.

Ear

Earmark — (*to reserve*). We have earmarked a room for guests in our new house.

Ear-shot — (*hearing distance*). He stood within ear-shot.

To give one's ear — (*to attend*). Please give me your ear for a minute and I shall relate the whole affair to you.

Having itching ear — (*to be desirous of hearing novelties*). Old ladies have itching ears.

Over head and ears — (*deeply involved*). I am over head and ears in debt.

A word in one's ear — (*in private*). The departing husband wanted to have a word in the ears of his wife.

Lend an ear — (*to listen*). Countrymen ! Lend me your ears and I will tell you how to win freedom.

Turn a deaf ear — (*to refuse to listen*). I wanted to drive slowly, but the driver turned a deaf ear to me and met with an accident.

To have a person's ear — (*to create a favourable impression*). You have a person's ear.

Walls have ears — (*there may be listeners behind the walls*). Please do not speak loudly; even walls have ears.

Early

Early and late — (*at all times*). My friends are most welcome to visit me early and late.

The early bird get the worm — (*one who starts early is more successful*).

To keep early hours — (*to rise and go to bed early*). To keep early hours is a good habit.

To come to an early grave — (*to die untimely*). Raja's father came to an early grave.

Earnest

Earnest money — (*money advanced as security*). The Chief Engineer has demanded earnest money with the tenders submitted to him.

Earth

Earth-worm — (*grovelling person*). No one admires on earth-worm.

Easy

Easy-going — (*indolent, involved to comforts*). The old princes generally had an easy-going life.

Easy come, easy go — (*money acquired without efforts is spent thoughtlessly*).

Easy money — (*bribe*). Many policemen are making easy money now-a-days.

Take it easy — (*not to be in a hurry*). You have to finish this job within one year, so take it easy.

Ill at ease — (*uncomfortable*). Your impolite behaviour makes me very much ill at ease.

Easy and free — (*not strict*). Our officer is easy and free.

Easy circumstances — (*affluence*). You are a man of easy circumstances.

Easy virtue — (*loose character*). The girl in question is of easy virtue.

Eat

To eat one's word — (*to retrace one's words in a humiliating manner*). When I protested he ate his words.

To eat humble pie — (*to have to apologise; to be humiliated*). Do not be arrogant lest you may have to eat the humble pie very soon.

To eat away — (*to destroy gradually*). Rust has eaten away the wooden door.

Eat the air — (*to be deluded with hopes*). I had to eat the air, when he refused to help me.

To eat up — (*to consume*). Smoking is eating up many young men.

To eat one's heart out — (*to suffer silently*). While in love one has to eat his heart out.

Echo

To cheer to the echo (*to cheer loudly; to applaud most heartily*). Wherever she went, Mother Teresa was cheered to the echo.

Economy

Economy of truth — (*falsehood*). Your letter enjoys economy of truth.

Edge

To be on edge — (*to be excited*). It is indecent to be always on edge.

To take the edge off — (*to make blunt; ineffective*). You are taking the edge off your argument.

Effect

To leave no effects — (*to die without any property*). The deceased left no effects; his wife is therefore in a pitiable condition.

To give effect to — (*to make operative*). The subordinate staff is expected to give effect to the orders of their superior officer.

Take effect —(*to come into force*). The Emergency Law would take effect immediately.

Egg

In the egg — (*in an early stage*). Our social reforms are still in the egg.

A bad egg — (*a worthless scheme or person*). An unplanned turns out to be a bad egg.

A good egg — (*excellent person or scheme*). The Janata Life Policy Scheme is a good egg.

To egg on — (*to induce*). He egged on me to insult you.

Elbow

At one's elbow — (*close at hand*). We and our friends are at our elbow in prosperity.

Up to the elbow — (*completely engrossed*). Sudesh is up to the elbow in his studies and cannot spare even a minute.

Out at elbow — (*poor*). For the last five years I have been out of elbow.

Element

To be in one's element — (*to be in agreeable company or work*). A clerk cannot be in his element in a merchant's shop.

War of elements — (*great storm*). In Fiji Island there has been a war of elements.

Out of elements — (*minus natural happiness*). He was out of elements during the marriage.

Elephant

A white elephant — (*a burdensome possession*). A motor-car is a white elephant for many these days.

Elixir

Elixir of life — (*a drug for prolonging life*). Good health is the best elixir of life.

Eleventh

Eleventh hour — (*the very last moment*). You cannot do every thing at the eleventh hour.

Elf

Elflock — (*a tangled lock of hair*). My wife has an elegant elflock.

Elf struck — (*bewitched*). That lady elf struck me completely.

Embark

Embark — (*start*). I would embark in a business soon.

Embargo

Under the embargo — (*under impediment*). Our whole business is under the embargo.

Employ

In the employ of — (*employed by*). I am in the employ of A.S. High School, Ambala.

Empty

Empty-handed — (*bringing no gift*). He came back from his friend's house empty-handed.

Empty compliment — (*a hollow compliment; without warmth*). Our political leaders are in the habit of paying empty compliments.

Come away empty — (*to come away without receiving anything*). He will come away empty from the University.

End

No end — (*without any limit*). There is no end to knowledge.

Odd and ends — (*miscellaneous things*). He told me about the odds and ends of his business.

Place on ends — (*upright*). Place the newspapers on ends.

To gain ends — (*to find purpose*). You must work hard to gain ends.

World without end — (*for ever*). We wanted the world without end.

Come to an end — (*become useless*). My motor engine has come to and end.

To be the end of — (*to cause the death of*). This mischievous baby will be the end of her mother.

At loose ends — (*in disorder, unoccupied*). You may meet me when I am at loose ends.

In the end — (*finally*). In the end let me pay my thanks to you for your cordial hospitality.

To make both ends meet — (*to balance one's expenditure to one's income*). Due to rise in the prices it has become quite difficult to make both ends meet.

To put to an end — (*to stop*). Lawlessness among students must be put to an end.

To gain one's own ends — (*to satisfy one's own selfish purpose*). Some people do help only to gain their own ends.

Keep one's ends up — (*to acquaint oneself well*). You must your ends up in the world.

Turn end for end — (*reverse*). Please turn the magazine end for end.

To end in smoke — (*to come to nothing*). All his efforts ended in smoke.

Enemy

The last enemy — (*the death*). The last enemy awaits the return of everybody.

Engrave

Engrave upon one's heart — (*to leave a permanent impression*). Shri Nehru's words are engraved upon my heart.

Engross

Engrossed into — (*completely absorbed*). He is engrossed into his studies.

Enough

Enough and to spare — (*in sufficient quantity*). I have money enough and to spare.

Enter

Enter into — (*to become a party to; to be interested in; engage*). He entered into agreement with me.

Enter upon — (*to engage in*). When are you entering upon your new business ?

To enter the field — (*to come forward, to complete*). Quite a large number of candidates have entered the field.

Equal

To have no equal — (*to be without rival*). So far as tragic acting is concerned, Meena Kumari has no equal.

Equal to the occasion — (*fit for any emergency*). Indian army has proved their equal to the occasion in the recent Pakistani aggression.

Epoch

Epoch-making — (*a period remarkable for improvement*). We are all living in an epoch-making era.

Errand

To make an errand — (*to invent a reason for going*). He made an errand to meet his wife.

A fool's errand — (*a useless undertaking*). One should not take up a fool's errand.

To go on an errand — (*To go with a message*). He went on an errand to the Prime Minister.

Error

Writ of error — (*reversal of judgement*). We secured a writ of error from the High Court.

Escape

Escape literature — (*light reading*). Fiction is merely an escape literature.

To escape one's notice — (*not to come within observation*). This error escaped my notice.

Estate

Fourth estate — (*press*). In democracy the fourth estate is the first requirement.

Eve

On the eve of — (*at the time of*). He worked hard on the eve of the examination.

Daughter of the Eve — (*woman*). The daughter of the eve is an essential part of the universe.

Born of eve — (*every human being*). Very few born of eve can resist the temptation of food.

Even

Even-handed — (*just*). I have distributed the profits even-handed.

Even money — (*neither laying nor taking odds equally*). I bet the odds were even money.

Even-minded — (*possessing a calm mind*). My mother is an even-minded lady.

Be even with — (*have one's revenge upon*). At last he was even with me.

Evening

The evening star — (*decline*). It is now the evening star of her beauty.

The evening of life — (*old age*). My father is enjoying now the evening of life.

Ever

The Ever-lasting — (*God*). The Ever-lasting knows better.

Ever and anon — (*now and then*). Please do remember us ever and anon.

Ever green — (*always green; always fresh*). The recollections of your kindness shall remain ever green in my mind.

Every

Every now and then — (*from time to time*). She visits my place every now and them.

Evil

Speak evil of — (*to slander*). Do not speak evil of any person in his absence.

An evil-minded — (*wicked*). Beware of evil-minded persons.

The evil one — (*the devil*). The evil one is always unkind to the lazy person.

Example

To set a good example — (*to create precedent*). Our leaders should themselves set good examples in serving the people; others will naturally follow.

Take example by — (*copy*). Take an example by following Bal.

To make an example — (*to punish*). The court should make an example of Man Singh.

Exception

To make an exception to — (*to object*). He took exception to my remarks.

Exception proves the rule — (*the existence of exception proves that the rule exists*).

Without an exception — (*all*). The law of the land applies to all without any exception.

With the exception of — (*except*). Every boy will attend the party with the exception of Anand.

Excess

In excess — (*more than*). You have money in excess.

Exchange

In exchange of — (*in return*). You may take my book in exchange of your pen.

Exhibition

To make an exhibition of one's self — (*to behave foolishly*). Try to behave decently and do not make an exhibition of yourself any more.

Ex-officio

Ex-officio — (*by virtue of one's office*). The head of the office is ex-officio chairman of the office's staff council.

Expense

At the expense of — (*at the cost of*). To earn money at the expense of one's health is a poor bargain.

Explosive

High explosive — (*very irritable man*). Your youngest brother is a high explosive.

An explosive situation — (*a situation which may burst out any time*). An explosive situation has developed in South-East Asia, due to the presence of United State's warships.

Express

An express wish — (*an ardent desire*). It was an express wish of Mr. Nehru that his ashes should be scattered over the fields of India.

Express bullet — (*fast danger*). NATO is an express bullet from imperialist countries.

Extent

A vast extent of marsh — (*useless stuff*). The manifesto of the communalist parties in India is a vast extent of marsh.

To a great extent — (*for the most part of it*). You are responsible to a great extent for that error.

Extreme

In the extreme — (*highest degree*). You have a dullard in the extreme.

go to the extreme — (*to go to far*). Our group leader advised us that we should not go to the extreme and decide the issue by mutual discussion.

The last extremity — (*utmost misfortune*). Sudama had reached the last extremity when Lord Krishna came forward to help him.

Eye

To catch the eye of someone — (*to attract the attention of somebody*). Her captivating beauty caught the eye of someone in the college.

To set one's eye on — (*to behold; to see*). The moment I set my eye on her, I was bewitched by her charms.

To open a person's eye — (*to show something of which a person has no knowledge*). The Chinese aggression over a peaceful country like India has opened the eyes of the world.

To pipe one's finger in the eye — (*to weep*). Baby, please do not pipe your finger in your eye.

To keep an eye on — (*keep watch on*). Please keep an eye on my books in my absence.

Eye for eye — (*retaliation*). Eye for eye leads to enmity.

To make one open one's eyes — (*to stare with astonishment*). Defeat made him open his eyes.

Have an eye on — (*have as one's object*). Beware of Krishan, he has an eye on your money.

In the eyes of law — (*from law point*). This contract is void in the eyes of law.

In the mind's eye — (*in imagination*). One may do anything in one's mind's eye.

Throw dust in the eyes — (*deceive*). One cannot always throw dust in the eyes of others.

Apple of one's eyes — (*very dear*). This baby is the apple of everybody's eyes in the family.

With a jealous eye — (*jealously*). Let us not watch the success of our friends with a jealous eye.

See eye to eye — (*agree entirely*). India and Pakistan do not see eye to eye on the Kashmir problem.

Eyewash — (*bunkum*). All peace propaganda by big powers is an eyewash.

Eye-witness — (*one who is present on the scene and watches a thing done*). An eye-witness is the keystone of the evidence required to prove any criminal charge upon a man.

Eye-shot — (*within seeing distance*). Please do remain within in eye-shot so that I could call you.

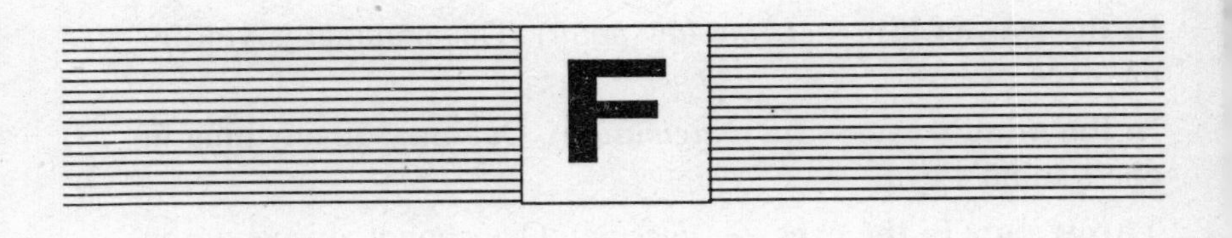

Face

To show one's face — (*to appear*). Since he got married, he has seldom shown his face here.

To pull a long face — (*to look discontented or disappointed*). When I refused to help him, he pulled a long face.

To put on a good face — (*to assume a contented face*). Despite poverty I always put on a good face.

To look in the face — (*to be bold*). To look in the face of one's enemy is a reflection of boldness.

In the face of — (*despite*). Porus fought bravely in the face of so many odds.

To make faces — (*to grimace*). Do not make faces at your elders.

Face to face — (*in actual presence, confronted*). Many misunderstandings are removed by face-to-face talk.

To face the music — (*to face the consequences*). One has to face the music of his deeds.

To put a new face on — (*to alter the aspect of*). The death of Mr. Nehru has put a new face on India's foreign policy.

To lose face — (*to be humiliated*). He has lost face among his friends.

On the face of it — (*to judge by appearance*). He looks honest on the face of it.

Fact

As a matter of fact — (*in reality*). As a matter of fact no one likes the Chemistry Professor of our college.

The fact of the matter — (*simple truth about the subject under reference*). The fact of the matter is that he was promoted out of turn.

Fag

Fag end — (*useless remnant*). To serve a guest at the fag end of the tables is contrary to good manners.

Fail

Without fail — (*certainly*). I will meet him without fail.

Fair

Fair and square — (*honest*). We should always be fair and square in our deals.

Fair sex — (*ladies*). The fair sex should always be fair and square in their dealings.

Fair play — (*no cheating*). Let us adopt fair play in everything.

Fair trade — (*the principle of reciprocity in the free trade*). The trade today may be free but it certainly is not fair.

Fair means — (*honestly*). He won the name by fair means.

A fair hand — (*writing which can be easily read*). Prem has a fair hand.

One's fair fame — (*good name*). Gandhiji will always enjoy his fair fame throughout the whole world.

Fair promise — (*good chance*). There appears to be a fair promise of profit in this business.

Fair-weather friends — (*not good in need*). Keep away from fair-weather friends.

All is fair in love and war — (*all methods used in love or war can be justified*).

Fairy

Fairy tale — (*an incredible tale*). His love story is nothing but a fairy tale.

Faith

To pin one's faith upon — (*to depend*). I am pinning my faith upon you.

In good faith — (*with sincerity*). He told me all this in good faith.

Fall

To fall a prey — (*to become a victim*). You just fell a prey to his advice.

To fall out — (*to quarrel*). Friends should not fall out.

To fall in with — (*meet*). I fell in with Surinder

To fall flat — (*to produce no effect*). My advise fell flat on him.

To fall in with — (*agree*). I do not fall in with your views.

To fall out of — (*give up*). Do not fall out of your hope.

To fall short — (*to become insufficient*). The sugar is falling short day by day.

Fame

House of ill fame — (*house of prostitutes*). Never visit any house of ill fame.

False

To be in a false position — (*to become the cause of a person being misunderstood*).

To play false — (*to act deceitfully*). The customer has played the shopkeeper false.

Family

In a family way — (*in domestic manner*). A wise is one who settles everything in a family way.

Fancy

To take fancy to — (*to love : to take interest*). The young girl took a fancy for the prince.

To catch the fancy of — (*to please*). My cycle caught the fancy of my friends.

Far

Far between — (*infrequent*). My visits are far between.

Far-sighted — (*seeing to a great distance*). My old father is a far-sighted man.

Far-reaching — (*widely applicable*). This is my far-reaching plan.

Far-fetched — (*having distant meaning*). His words are far-fetched.

Far cry — (*a long distance away*). Socialism in this country is as yet a far cry.

In so far as — (*to the extent of*). In so far as I am concerned you can be sure of my help.

Fast

Fast friend — (*bosom friend*). Both of them are fast friends.

Hard and fast — (*definite*). There are no hard and fast rules in international politics.

Play fast and loose — (*to be unreliable*). None can be sure of your help, because you always play fast and loose.

Fast with gout — (*confined*). You fast with gout.

Fat

The fat is in the fire — (*there will be an explosion*)

Fat-headed	
Fat-brained	dull, stupid
Fat-witted	

Fatal

Fatal blow — (*a blow which causes death*). He struck his enemy with a fatal *lathi* blow.

Fatal thread — (*allotted length of life*). All of us hang by the fatal thread.

Father

Father of the nation — (*greatest leader*). Gandhi is called the Father of the Nation.

Fawn

To fawn on — (*to flatter*). The children fawn on their parents.

Fear

Without fear and favour — (*impartially*). We must do our duty without fear and favour.

Feather

In high feather — (*full of spirits*). They are in high feather.

Show white feather — (*to betray; cowardice*). Bhagat Singh was a person who never showed the white feather.

A feather in one's cap — (*something to be proud of*). This award is another feather in your cap.

Birds of same feather flock together — (*persons belonging to the same class work or think alike*).

To feather one's own nest — (*to enrich onself*). Everyone is trying to feather his own nest.

Feel

To feel the pulse — (*to find out one's secret opinion*). Before taking any decision in respect of my brother's marriage, my daddy would like to feel his pulse.

To feel at home — (*to feel easy*). All of us should try to make the foreign tourists feel at home while they are in India.

Fiddle

Fit as a fiddle — (*in good condition*). Rajaji is still fit as a fiddle.

To play the second fiddle — (*to perform a secondary purpose*). A sincere social worker would always be ready to play the second fiddle.

To play the first fiddle — (*to take a leading part*). Mr. Sohan rightly deserves to play the first fiddle in every national movement.

To fiddle faddle — (*to trifle*). It never pays to fiddle faddle in our duties.

Field

Fair field and no favour — (*equal conditions in contest*). Let our job be a fair field and no favour.

Fig

To care a fig (*not to care*). I care a fig for your advice.

Figure

To cut a sorry figure — (*to be ridiculed*). The president cut a sorry figure in the hall.

Person of figure — (*man of distinction*). In the world of literature Bernard Shaw will remain a person of figure.

File

File with — (*to be equal*). General Giani files with any other military expert deputed to the United Nations.

Find

To find one's legs — (*to rise; to stand up*). When the drunkard found his legs he noticed that he has been lying on the road.

Finger

To look through one's fingers — (*to pretend not to see*). At times the teacher has to look through his fingers.

My finger itch — (*I am impatient*).

To have a finger in the pie — (*to interfere in something*). I have no finger in the pie of your marriage.

To the finger-nails — (*completely*). He is under debt to the finger-nails.

On one's finger-tips — (*to be well-versed in*). He has all the data at his finger-tips.

To burn one's finger — (*to get into unexpected trouble*). You have burnt your fingers in that speculative deal and today you are penniless.

Finish

To fight to a finish — (*to fight till the end of death*). our Jawans shall always fight to a finish.

Fire

On fire — (*excited*). Please discuss this issue peacefully, do not be on fire.

Fire up — (*to fly into passion*). Hardly had I uttered this word than he fired up and began to beat me.

Fire out — (*to dismiss*). Fire out this servant, he is dishonest.

Fire away — (*begin*). Fire away with your work immediately.

Between two fires — (*between two difficulties*). Sometimes circumstances put us between two fires.

Fire and sword — (*burning and slaughter*). The history of heroes is full of fire and sword.

Set the Thames on fire — (*do something remarkable*). It is high time that you should set the Thames on fire.

To pour oil on fire — (*being accused; being blamed*). The President's speech poured oil on fire.

To add fuel to the fire — (*to add insult to the injury*). His father's remarks after his failure in the test added fuel to the fire.

First

First come, first served — (*to be obliged on one's turn*).

From first to last — (*throughout*). She stood by me from first to last.

First and the foremost — (*the most important*). The first and the foremost things for you is to learn typing.

Fish

A fish out of water — (*a person who feels uncomfortable in his surroundings*). When in Pakistan I felt like a fish out of water.

Pretty kettle of fish — (*confusion*). Our office is a pretty kettle of fish.

To fish in troubled waters — (*to do things under unhelpful circumstances*). By intervening in Indo-Pak relations, China is trying to fish in troubled waters.

Other fish to fry — (*more important work to attend to*). Please be brief in your expression, I have other fish to fry.

Fit

Fits and starts — (*irregularly*). We should work regularly and not by fits and starts.

Fit out — (*equipped*). The train is fitted out for the tour.

Flame

To fan the flames — (*to make it more intense*). Your speech would fan the flames of disturbances.

To burst into flames — (*to burn with a glow*). The van carrying explosives burst into flames.

An old flame — (*sweetheart*). Sundari is an old flame of mine.

Flee

Flee for one's life — (*to run away in order to save anothers life*). Many good hearted persons had to flee for their lives during the crisis.

Flesh

Flesh and fell — (*the whole body*). The flesh and fell is subject to decay.

Fleshy-minded — (*given to pleasures of senses only*). The era of fleshy-minded kings is over.

One's flesh and blood — (*close relationship*). She is my own flesh and blood.

To put on flesh — (*to become fat*). Happiness is the best thing to put on flesh.

All flesh — (*all human beings*). All flesh must die one day.

Floor

To take the floor — (*to speak in debate*). The minister took the floor.

To floor the paper — (*to answer question in it*). The Prime Minister floored the paper.

Flow

Flow with milk and honey — (*full of prosperity*). India once flowed with milk and honey.

Flow of soul — (*genial conversation*). I always enjoy a flow of soul with Prema.

Flower

A flowery style — (*a style of writing in which figures of speech abound*). Sahir has a flowery style of writing verses.

The flower of age — (*youth*). Our students are the flowers of age of our nation.

Fly

A fly on wheel — (*a person who over-estimates his powers*). Our next door country is a mere fly on wheel.

To fly high — (*to be ambitious*). Let us not fly high but proceed according to the facts of life.

To fly at — (*to rush upon suddenly, attack*). The dog flew at the thief's throat.

High flown — (*extravagant bombastic*). Please do not talk in high flown terms.

To fly out — (*to burst into violent words*). Please behave yourself; do not fly out.

The bird is flown — (*the wanted man has escaped*). It is no use chasing him now; the bird has flown already.

To fly to arms — (*to take up arms*). Freedom makes Africans fly to arms.

To fly upon — (*to seize upon; to attack*). The Nagas have stopped flying upon the Indian army now-a-days.

Fog

In fog — (*puzzled*). My future is in fog.

Follow

To follow in the footsteps of — (*to follow the example*). Shri Shastri had decided to follow in the footsteps of late Shri Nehru.

Follow out — (*pursue to the end*). Follow your ambitions out.

Food

Food for thought — (*something which affords an occasion to think*). The death of my wife has given me enough food for thought.

Fool

To make a fool of — (*to make a fun of*). People made a fool of him.

Be a fool to — (*nothing in comparison*). I am a fool to Rashid.

No fool like an old fool — (*lovers are always foolish*).

Fool's paradise — (*illusory happiness*). His day dreams have made his life a fool's paradise.

Fool's bolt is soon shot — (*his stock of argument is soon over*).

Go on fool's errand — (*fruitless work*). In life most of us go on a fool's errand.

Foot

To have feet of clay — (*liable to be overthrown*). A political party always has feet of clay.

Know the length of one's foot — (*to know one's weakeness and manage it*). One should know the length of one's foot.

Have one foot in the grave — (*near death*). Our grand-mother has one foot in the grave.

To carry of his feet — (*to make him enthusiastic*). I carried him off his feet.

For

To take for better or worse — (*to accept for all circumstances*). I have taken his advise for better or worse.

For the better — (*indicates improvement*). The patient has taken a turn for the better.

Force

Force the pace — (*to hasten unduly*). If we want our country to be in tune with the West, we must force the pace of our progress.

Fortune

To make a fortune — (*to earn a lot*). He has made a fortune in the business.

To try one's fortune — (*to take a risky step*). Let us try our fortune and join in his business.

Foul

Through foul and fair — (*through everything*). You have now passed through foul and fair.

Foul play — (*dishonest dealing*). We should not indulge in a foul play with our friends.

Through fair and foul weather — (*through good and bad times*). She promised to live by me through fair and foul weather.

Fountain

A crown is the fountain of honour — (*all the honour belongs to the ruler*).

Fountain of justice — (*full justice*). The President of India is a fountain of justice.

Four

Four corners of the earth — (*anywhere; everywhere*). Let peace prevail in the four corners of the earth.

Frame

A proper frame of mind — (*in good mood*). Do not discuss my future at present; I am not in a proper frame of mind today.

Free

To have a free hand — (*to have complete liberty of action*). I have a free hand in managing the affairs of my company.

A free-lance — (*not directly connected with any organisation*) I am a free-lance journalist.

Fresh

Fresh lease of life — (*new scope for living*). His recovery from serious illness gave him a fresh lease of life.

In the fresh of morning — (*in the pleasant morning time*). We will meet in the fresh of morning.

From

From hand to mouth — (*to live within a little income*). Most of the working class people of India today are living from hand to mouth.

From door to door — (*from house to house*). I am selling my wares from door to door.

Full

In the fullness of time — (*at the proper time*). Had you availed yourself of the opportunity in the fullness of time, you would, today, have been a millionaire.

Gab

Gift of the Gab — (*a talent of talking*). Many women have a gift of the gab.

Gain

To gain ground — (*to succeed slowly and steadily*). He is working on the basis of gaining ground.

To gain time — (*to get time on some pretext; to make full preparations*). Today's statement of the Police Inspector will enable the criminal to gain time.

To gain one's point — (*to defeat opposition in argument*). It is very difficult to gain my sister's point.

Gaiter

Ready to the last gaiter button — (*completely ready*). Are you ready to the last gaiter button for today's performance ?

Gala

Gala day (*a happy holiday*). Sunday is always a gala day.

Galanty

Galanty show — (*shadow of puppets*). Life is nothing but a galanty show.

Gale

Hanging gale — (*arrears of rent*). He has not as yet cleared his hanging gale for the last three months.

Gall

In the gall of bitterness — (*in a state of hostility to God*). In the gall of bitterness even some sadhus start abusing.

To dip ones pen in gall — (*to write violently*). His dip of pen in gall brought him to.

Gall and wormwood — (*anything extremely disagreeable*). Would you please stop your gall and wormwood talk ?

Gallant

To play the gallant with — (*to flirt*). Narinder's habit of playing the gallant with college girls has disreputed his whole family.

Gallery

To play to the gallery — (*to appeal to the lower class*). Such movies are meant only to play to the gallery.

Gallop

To gallop through — (*to make quick progress*). You cannot get good marks just by galloping through books.

Gamble

To gamble away — (*to love*). He has gambled away all his property.

Game

The game is up — (*the scheme has failed*). Your game of making good money is up now.

To play a double game — (*to manage things cleverly*). If you want me to help you in this matter, please stop playing the double game.

To play one's game — (*to advance one's schemes*). At last Guptaji is now able to play his game.

Game and game — (*one victory scored by each side*). The hockey match has ended in game and game.

Gander

Sauce for the goose is sauce for the gander — (*What is good for one is also good for another*).

Gang

To gang up — (*to join*). The Inspector ordered the policemen to gang up.

Gaol

Gaol-bird — (*one who is frequently sent to prison*). Balwant is a gaol-bird on charges of cheating people.

Gap

To stop gap — (*to make up deficiency*). His hard labour enabled him to stop a gap in his studies.

Garb

A wolf in the garb of a lamb — (*a scoundrel in the dress of a saint*). Many a modern sadhu is a wolf in the garb of a lamb.

Garden

To lead up the garden path — (*to entice, to mislead*). If the leader leads up to the garden path, where will the public go ?

Gate

Gate crasher — (*uninvited intruder*). The Chinese were gate crashers in India in 1962.

To break gates — (*to enter college hostel after the prescribed hours*). Satish's habit of breaking gates was the cause of his being expelled from the hostel.

Gate of horn — (*by which true dreams come*). I don't know when I will pass through the gates of horn.

Between you and me and the gatepost — (*in close confidence*). Rest assured the talk we had will remain between you and me and the gatepost.

Gather

A rolling stone gathers no moss — (*a person who does not stick to one job never succeeds in life*).

To gather strength — (*to become strong*). The patient is gathering strength now.

To gather colour — (*to be brown*). Her face is gathering colour.

To gather away — (*to get headway*). The train has gathered away.

Gauge

Have the weather gauge of — (*have the advantage of*). He has the weather gauge of being intelligent.

To take the gauge of — (*to estimate*). Will you take the gauge of income and expenditure of last month.

Gauntlet

To run the gauntlet — (*to be exposed to unpleasant remarks or treatment*). Policemen have to run the gauntlet as much as to win applause of the people.

To throw down the gauntlet — (*to issue a challenge*). Let the youth of this country throw down the gauntlet to all anti-social elements to behave well in future.

To take up the gauntlet — (*to accept a challenge*). India is now in a position to take up the gauntlet with any country.

Gazing

Gazing stock — (*one who is exposed to public view*). The unnatural beauty of the young girl was the gazing stock of young people.

Gear

Out of gear — (*not working*). The car has gone out of gear.

In gear — (*in working order*). The car is in gear.

General

In general — (*generally*). In general women do not smoke.

Lover-general — (*one who makes love to every women*). Krishan is a lover-general.

Gentle

Gentle-folk — (*people of family*). Gentle-folk of our neighbour have gone out for picnic.

Gentleman at large — (*a carefree person without any employment*). Narinder is a gentleman at large.

Gentleman's agreement — (*moral agreement*). Let us have a gentleman's agreement that we shall all try our best to co-operate with each other in times of crisis.

The old gentleman — (*the devil*). The old gentleman of U.P. is in Delhi now.

Gesture

A friendly gesture — (*an expression of friendship*). In inviting the Prime Minister of England to visit India, the Indians have made a friendly gesture.

Get

To get rid of — (*to leave*). I want to get rid of my wife at all costs.

To get into a scrape — (*to get into an unexpected trouble*). By going to Pakistan my brother got into a scrape.

To get into — (*put on*). Let's get into the bargain.

To get round — (*to evade*). One who tries to get round the income tax falls in trouble one day.

To get a chance for the better — (*to improve*). The patient has got a chance for the better.

To get through — (*to pass*). I am sure he will get through in his final examination.

To get along — (*to advance*). The scheme seems sound. He can get along with it.

Get-up — (*the style of production*). The get-up of our books has been liked by all our readers.

Get a move on — (*start*). Can we get a move on with this now ?

To get on — (*to live together*). The relations between them are so strained that the husband and wife cannot get on well now.

To get at — (*to reach*). We are trying to get at the peak of this hill.

Ghost

To give up the ghost — (*to die*). The old lady gave up the ghost last night.

Ghost of a chance — (*a very light chance*). He has only ghost of a chance to get the job.

Our ghostly enemy — (*the devil*). Beware of the ghostly enemy.

Ghostly weapons — (*religious arguments*). You cannot win her confidence just by ghostly weapons.

Giddy

Giddy success — (*bewildering*). Politics soon brought him giddy success.

Gift

Gift of the gab — (*power of taking*). Ladies generally have the gift of the gab.

Gild

Gild the bill — (*to cover over a disagreeable thing*). For some, marriage is a gilded pill.

Ginger

Ginger shall be hot in the mouth — (*the love of pleasure is immortal*).

Ginger-bread work — (*cheap and showy ornamental work*). She is wearing ginger-bread work.

Gird

To gird up one's loins — (*to prepare for action*). The aggressors are girding up their loins.

Give

To give way — (*to fall*). The tree has given way in the storm.

To give up the ghost — (*to die*). The old lady gave up the ghost last night.

To give in — (*to yield*). Let us give in to come to some conclusion.

To give chase — (*to pursue*). Who will give chase to the problem ?

To give place to — (*to give one's place to someone else*). We have given that place to his brother.

To give the world — (*punish*). The Prime Minister's statement has given the world.

To give oneself airs — (*to feel proud*). My father-in-law has given his airs for wealth.

The give-and-take policy — (a fair measure of policy on both sides). Success in the modern world depends on the give-and-take policy.

Glamour

To cast a glamour over — (*to enchant*). The young actresses cast a glamour over the youth.

Glance

To glance at — (*to make ironical remarks*). The teacher glanced at students.

Glove

Hand and glove — (*bosom friends*). Pushpa and Sarla are hand and glove.

To fit like a glove — (*exactly*). Today's statement of the Prime Minister fits like a glove to our national policy.

Glut

Glut in the market — (*supply in excess of demand*). In the rainy season vegetables glut the market.

Go

To go halves (*to share equally in profit and loss*). We brothers are going halves in business.

To go the way of all earth — (*die*). The old man has gone the way of all earth this morning.

To go rack and ruin — (*to be completely ruined*). As a result of fire the whole market has gone to rack and ruin.

To go hand in hand — (*complete agreement*). On the issue of 'rice production in the country' all the ministers went hand in hand.

To go up the line — (*leave the base for the front*). The Indian Army has gone up the line in NEFA.

To go about — (*from place to place*). For getting orders, he goes about the whole city.

To go through — (*to examine*). The examiner has gone through the answer books throughly.

To go over — (*to inspect*). The police inspector has been advised to go over the report of the murder.

Go on — (*continue*). Go on with your statement, please.

At the first go — (*at the very start*). Shamsher was leading the race in the first go.

To go under — (*to be called by some title*). Krishna Malik goes under the assumed name of 'Dalip'.

To go to great expenses — (*to spend a lot*). He is going to great expenses in business now-a-days.

God

God's book — (*the Bible*). God's book is read in every church.

God of this world — (*the devil*). Atom is another God of this world.

God'. forsaken — (*miserable*). The patient is God'-forsaken.

God's acre — (*graveyard*). The corpse lies in God's acre.

Gold

Gold fever — (*desire for money*). Human weakness in gold fever.

A golden age — (*a prosperous period of history*). The golden age has passed from the modern world now.

Gold digger — (*one who is bent upon making money through all means*). A village bania in India is a gold digger.

Golden opportunity — (*very favourable chance*). We have got golden opportunity of starting a new business now.

Gone

Gone under — (*ruined*). My uncle has completely gone under.

A gone man — (*hopeless*). The new clerk possesses a gone man personality.

Good

To be as good as one's word — (*to keep one's promise*). You can rely upon him to be as good as his word.

For good — (*for ever*). We have left Pakistan for good.

A good hand at — (*clever in doing*). He is a good hand at watch repairing.

Good for nothing — (*useless*). That fellow is good for nothing.

To get into good graces — (*to obtain one's friendship*). At last he was able to get into good graces of that man.

Good money — (*genuine*). Your earning by honest means is always good money.

Goose

All his goose are swans — (*he overestimates*). Sudesh's all goose are swans.

To kill the goose that lays golden eggs — (*to sacrifice future profits*). I do not want to kill the goose that lays golden eggs by selling my book at cheap rates.

Got

Got-up — (*artificially produced*). The got-up statements stand nowhere.

Grab

Have the grab on — (*have great advantage of*). He has the grab on Malhotra's influence in getting a job.

Grace

To fall from grace — (*to cease to be in one's good books*). The clerk has fallen from the grace of his manager.

With good grace — (*willingly*). I have left the job with a good grace.

Airs and graces — (*behaviour*). It's high time that you should change your bad airs and graces.

To be in one's good grace — (*to be in one's good books*). The clerk is in the good graces of his manager.

Grade

On the up-grade — (*progressing*). The patient is on the up-grade now-a-days.

Grade up — (*improve*). Please grade up the quality of your products.

To make the grade — (*to succeed*). He will make the grade in the examination.

Grain

Against the grain — (*contrary to inclination*). You cannot except good work from your workers if you compel them to work against the grain.

Grape

Grapes from thorns — (*good from bad*). He has the art of getting grapes from thorns.

Grapple

To grapple with — (*to tackle*). It is difficult to grapple with the problem arising from high cost of living.

Grasp

Out of one's grasp — (*beyond one's reach*). Boys are out of Manu's grasp.

Grasp at — (*to catch at*). His efforts to grasp at the running train failed.

Grave

With one foot in the grave — (*about to die*). The patient of Ward No. 10 is with one foot in the grave.

To dig one's grave — (*to bring ones ruin*). You are going to dig your own grave by starting this business.

Quiet as the grave — (*quiet*). During curfew a town becomes as quiet as the grave.

Grease

To grease one's palm — (*to bribe*). The habit of greasing one's palm is expanding in our country like anything.

Like greased lightning — (*very fast*). The aeroplane disappeared like greased lightning.

Great

A great gun — (*a man of note*). The Professor of Chemistry in our college is a great gun now-a-days.

Greek

Greek gift — (*one given with intent of harming*). At last he succeeded in giving his Greek gift to Pushpa.

Green

Green eye — (*jealousy*). Your green eyes will ruin you one day.

A green horn — (*a raw fellow*). The new clerk is absolutely a green horn.

Grind

To grind one's own axe — (*to serve one's self-interest*). Surekha is in the habit of grinding her own axe.

Grip

To lose one's grip — (*to lose control*). The grandfather has lost grip on his youngest grandson.

Ground

To hold one's ground — (*to stand firm*). Unless you improve your habits, you cannot hold your ground.

Gun

As sure as gun — (*quite sure*). He is as sure as gun to get first class in his examination.

To blow great guns — (*said of a storm blowing fiercely*). Last night the rains blew great guns.

Gutter

Gutter-press — (*press catering to vulgar tastes*). A gutter-press in any country cannot thrive for long.

Habeas corpus

Habeas corpus petition — (*a writ for the production in court of prisoner*). Many political prisoners often invoke habeas corpus petitions.

Habit

Habit of mind — (*mental constitution*). Something or the other is always a habit of mind in every human being.

To get into a habit — (*to become habitual*). His hobby of drinking has resulted in getting into bad habit.

Hail

To hail from — (*to come from*). Our manager hails from America.

Within hail distance — (*near enough to be called*). He is standing within hail distance.

Hair

Hair breadth escape — (*very narrow escape*). During partition my brother had a hair breadth escape.

Against the hair — (*not pleasant*). I don't want anything against the hair.

To a hair — (*exactly*). I am going to build my house to a hair like my brother's.

To get a person by the short hair — (*have complete control over him*). Parents should get children by the short hair.

Half

Half-hearted — (*lacking courage*). Half-hearted efforts are never successful.

To do things by halves — (*imperfectly*). Many labourers of our factory are doing things by halves.

Half-baked — (*inexperienced*). The half-baked clerk has been dismissed from service.

Too clever by half — (*very clever*). Manmohan is too clever by half in his work.

Better half — (*wife*). My better-half has gone to Mumbai.

To meet half way — (*to compromise*). The only solution to their difference is that they should meet halfway.

To get half a nelson on — (*to hold complete control*). Parents should get half a nelson on their children.

Half-mast — (*half-flown flag*). Due to the death of the Prime Minister, the flags in the country are flying half-mast.

Hall

Hallmark — (*important feature*). Today's statement of the Prime Minister is a hallmark of the Government's policy.

Halt

Halt between two opinions — (*hesitate*). Do not half between two opinions in telling the truth.

Hammer

Knight of the hammer — (*blacksmith*). The knight of the hammer of our village died this morning.

To hammer an idea into one's head — (*to make one understand*). It is very difficult to hammer an idea into Rama's head.

Hand

A bird in hand — (*any advantage held at present*). A bird in hand is better than two in the bush.

At hand — (*close by*). His house is at hand to mine.

To take off one's hand — (*to relieve one of something troublesome*). By starting his business he has taken off his hands from service.

Pass through many hands — (*share in action*). This book has passed through many hands.

Hand and glove — (*fast friends*). Mohan and Sohan are hand and glove.

Hand down — (*succeed*). Today's paper was very difficult, many students will not hand down in the same.

From hand to mouth — (*poverty*). With this small income we are living from hand to mouth now-a-days.

Under one's hand — (*under one's signature*). The thieves were able to draw all the money from the bank under the manager's hand.

To take in hand — (*to undertake*). It is high time that you should take in hand the responsibility of your parents.

Out of hand — (*out of control*). His children have gone out of his hand.

On hand — (*ready; available*). I have only Rs. 20 on hand.

Off hand — (*immediately*). I cannot give any decision off hand. I must have some time to think over the problem.

On all hands — (*on all sides*). The Chinese were attacking on all hands.

To have clean hands — (*to be honest*). You cannot have clean hands in any office.

From good hands — (*from reliable source*). We have come to know from good hands that a few posts of clerks are lying vacant under control.

Come to hand — (*to receive*). All the members of my family came to hand at the railway station this morning.

To bear a hand — (*to take part in*) He is bearing a hand in games this time.

Hand to hand — (*close quarters*). The new military camps are going to be hand to hand.

Handsome

To feel handsome — (*to feel well*). The patient is feeling handsome.

Know a handsome or two — (*be experienced about*). I know a handsome or two of government jobs.

Hang

To get the hang of a thing — (*to understand a thing*). We cannot get the hang of your statement.

Hang over one's head — (*to be in danger*). The whole country is hanging over its head owing to increased cost of living.

To hang together — (*to keep united*). Come what may, we shall hang together.

To hang in the balance — (*undecided*). One who always hangs in the balance never succeeds.

To hang heavy — (*become burdensome*). The new job is hanging heavy on my head.

Hanky-panky

Hanky-panky — (*trickery*). Gogia Pasha is world famous for his hanky-panky.

Hard

Hard nut to crack — (*difficult problem to solve*). How to increase food production in our country is a hard nut to crack.

Hard of hearing — (*somewhat deaf*). His uncle is hard of hearing since childhood.

Hard and fast — (*strict*). There is no hard and fast rule in becoming a member of the I.T. Union.

Hard up — (*in want*). I am hard up of money now-a-days.

Hard-headed — (*clear*). Our manager is a hard headed man.

Hare

To run with the hare and hunt with the hound — (*to keep on with both sides*). A wise man will always run with the hare and hunt with the hound.

Hark

To hark back — (*to revert*). Never hark back of your stand once taken.

Harness

To die in harness — (*to die at one's work*). The leaders who die in harness are worshipped till ages.

Hash

To make hash of — (*to spoil completely*). He has made a hash of his career by going after girls.

Settle a person's hash — (*make an end of*). I can settle a hash of my friend only when he is willing to act on my advice.

Hat

Pass round the hat — (*to beg for collection*). The whole government is passing round the hat for building a fresh Prime Minister's Fund.

To talk through one's hat — (*boast*). He simply talks through his hat. In fact he is worth nothing.

Bad hat — (*dishonourable person*). What is the life of a bad hat ?

To send round the hat — (*to solicit contributions*). Let us send round the hat for orphans.

Hatchet

To bury the hatchet — (*to end the fight*). Will both of you now bury the hatchet and compromise?

To throw the hatchet — (*exaggerate*). Many women are in the habit of throwing the hatchet.

Have

Haves and have-nots — (*rich and poor*). All haves and have-nots sitting in this gathering are requested to contribute something for the Church Building Fund.

Have away — (*to remove*). Please have away your luggage from here.

Haven

Haven of peace — (*a peaceful retreat*). Never will a mortal find a heaven of peace earlier than this grave.

Havoc

To play havoc — (*to cause destruction*). A war always plays havoc.

Haw-Haw

Haw-haw — (*loud vulgar laughter*). I hate people making haw-haw.

Hawk

Hawk-eyed — (*keen sighted*). The old man of this village is hawk-eyed.

To know a hawk from the hacksaw — (*to be able to judge between things*). The art of knowing a hawk from a hacksaw is confined to few only.

Hay

Go haywire — (*to become excited*). He goes haywire with every young girl.

To make hay of — (*throw into confusion*). The Minister's statement has made hay of parliament's decision on planning in India.

Hazard

At all hazards — (*at all risks*). I am ready at all hazards to save the life of my wife.

Head

Cannot make a head or tail — (*cannot understand*). It is difficult to make a head or tail of the Prime Minister's today's speech.

To lose one's head — (*to be very much excited*). Do not lose your head if you want to have a solution on your family problems.

Good headed — (*talented*). He is a good-headed man.

Hot head — (*rash person*). A hot head is always a loser in life.

From head to foot — (*all over the body*). He is having pimples from head to foot.

Over head and ears — (*completely*). His father is involved in debt over head and ears.

Out of one's head — (*from one's invention*). The story I told you originally comes out of Satish's head.

At the head of — (*top*). Who is at the head of this council?

To put something in someone's head — (*suggest*). Many members of the club put something into the head of the leader to make Shri Gopal as their new secretary.

Come to a head — (*to reach climax*). Hema Malini has come to a head of her acting now-a-days.

To give the horse his head — (*let him go freely*). Will you please give the horse his head?

Heap

Heaps of time — (*much time*). Heaps of time is still left for our annual examination.

Knock all of a heap — (*to overthrow badly*). The Chinese knocked Indians all of a heap in 1962.

Heart

To have no heart — (*to have no feelings*). The old man of our street has no heart for his children.

After one's heart — (*to one's desire*). You can now do after your heart.

Heart-to-heart — (*frank and free*). Let us have heart-to-heart talk and finish the matter once for all.

Out of hearts — (*in low spirits*). It is but natural to be out of hearts when you fail in some examination.

Heart of oak — (*courageous man*). Alexander the Great had a heart of oak.

Break the heart — (*to die of grief etc*; *to be disappointed*). The man broke his heart for the misbehaviour of his family.

By heart — (*through memory*). I remember the whole story by heart.

Nearest one's heart — (*dearest*). Nearest to my heart is my wife.

To take a thing to heart — (*to be much affected by*). Don't take anything to heart about what she had said.

With all my heart — (*most willingly*). I apologise for my misbehaviour with all my heart.

Speak to the heart — (*to encourage*). Parents should always speak to the heart of their children for good manners.

Heart and soul — (*with all one's energy*). The whole government is working heart and soul to see the prosperity of the country.

Heart-and-hand — (*enthusiastically*). The pandit of the temple is working heart-and-hand for the welfare of the nation.

Heat

At a heat — (*in a simple effort*). You cannot succeed by working at a heat, take the help of your friends.

Heather

To set the heather on fire — (*to create a sensation*). The new taxation policy has set the heather on fire in the whole country.

To take to the heather — (*to become an outlaw*). Many take to the heather during riots.

Heaven

To be in the seventh heaven — (*to be extremely happy*). Even the richest person is not in a seventh heaven now-a-days.

Heaven of heavens — (*highest heavens*). May God let the soul of Pandit Nehru rest in heaven of heavens.

Heavy

Heavy news — (*sad news*). The whole world burst into tears on hearing the heavy news of the death of Mrs. Indira Gandhi.

Heel

On one's heels — (*close behind*). Please bring the file lying on my heels.

Heels overhead — (*upside down*). The child fell heels overhead.

To take to one's heels — (*to run away*). The thief took to his heels as soon as he saw the police.

Down at heels — (*miserable*). He is living in a down at heels condition now-a-days.

To show a clean pair of heels — (*to run off*). The thief showed a clean pair of heels in darkness.

To kick one's heels — (*to stand waiting*). He is kicking his heels for the last one hour for his friend.

Hell

Hell of noise — (*great noise*). The school students are making a hell of noise.

Helm

At the helm of affairs — (*those who control or are in authority*). The persons at the helm of any affair must be serious and patient.

Help

Help out — (*to extricate*). Please help me out of this difficulty.

It cannot be helped — (*nothing can be done in the matter*).

Help over — (*to enable to surmount*). Please help over the little boy in his studies.

Hen

Hen-hearted — (*coward*). The hen-hearted have no place in the army.

Here

Here and there — (*everywhere*). Although one cannot see but God is here and there.

Neither here nor there — (*nowhere or of no importance*). The facts given by him are neither here nor there.

Hey

Heyday — (*period of fullest vigour*). He gained everything during the heyday of his life.

Hide

To hide one's light under a bushel — (*to conceal*). No use hiding your light under a bushel, we know everything.

To play hide and seek — (*to deceive*). Never encourage the habit of playing hide-and-seek with your friends.

To hide one's head — (*to feel ashamed*). He is hiding his head after cheating us.

High

High time — (*time for action*). It is high time that you should realise your responsibility towards your parents.

High life — (*life of luxury*). The whole family of the Maharaja was leading a high life until his death.

High words — (*angry words*). High words are never appreciated.

High and low — (*rich and poor*). Every high and low sitting in this gathering is requested to contribute something towards the Chruch Building Fund.

High and Mighty — (*arrogant*). Tyrannical rulers are generally high and mighty.

High born — (*of high family*). Davinder is a high born boy.

Hilt

Up to the hilt — (*completely*). The proprietor of our company is in debt to the hilt.

Hinge

Off the hinge — (*in a state of confusion*). He being off the hinge, murdered his wife.

Hit

Hit upon — (*to come by chance*). He has hit upon a scheme.

To hit below the belt — (*to play foul*). His habit of hitting below the belt took him to prison.

To hit the nail on the head — (*to touch the exact point*). The police inspector was able to hit the nail on the thief's head.

Hit-off — (*to describe with typical strokes*). He hit off his wife this morning.

Hither

Hither and thither — (*here and there*). When I reached home I found all my things scattered hither and thither.

Hold

To hold one's own — (*to maintain one's position*). I cannot hold my own with Rs. 4,000 a month.

To hold over — (*to postpone*). Let us hold over the meeting till tomorrow.

To hold good — (*To apply*). A vehicle permit does not hold good everywhere in the country.

To hold out — (*to offer*). There is nothing good in our stock which we can hold out to you.

Hold off — (*to keep at a distance*). The thief warned; 'Hold off or else I will shoot you'.

To hold one's peace — (*to be silent*). The students in the class are holding their peace.

Hole

To pick holes in — (*to find fault with*). Will you please stop picking holes in the matter ?

Make holes in — (*use large amount of*). Women are in the habit of making holes in their husbands pockets.

Hollow

Hollow-hearted — (*insincere*). Hollow-hearted people are never successful in life.

Home

At home in — (*expert in*). Rajesh is at home in Mathematics.

At home — (*at ease*). Please be at home.

To bring home — (*to make one understand*). Unless we bring home Ramesh, we cannot convince other members.

Long home — (*grave*). Every one of us has to go to long home one day or the other.

Honest

To turn an honest penny — (*to earn a living honestly*). His father turned an honest penny throughout his life.

Honour

Word of honour — (*an honourable statement*). I believe in your word of honour.

Hook

By hook or by crook — (*by all means*). I must get this job by hook or by crook.

Off the hook — (*dead*). The baby went off the hook this morning.

On one's own book — (*on one's own account*). I may remind you once again all you are doing is on your own hook.

Hope

Hope against hope — (*to be hopeful even in the most despairing situations*). Every soldier has got to have hope against hope.

Horn

To take the bull by the horn — (*to face a problem boldly*). One must possess the courage of taking the bull by the horns.

On the horns of a dilemma — (*puzzled*). The death of my wife has left me on the horns of a dilemma.

To blow one's own horn — (*to boast*). Do something solid. No use blowing your own horn every now and then.

Hornet

To bring a hornet's nest about one's ears — (*to stir up trouble*). His brother is wise enough not to bring a hornet's nest about his ears.

Horse

To flog a dead horse — (*to try to revive a lost subject*). In trying to defend their territories, the Chinese are simply flogging the dead horse.

To work like a horse — (*to work hard*). If you want to get first position in your college, you will have to work like a horse.

To ride the high horse — (*to put on airs*). The success lies in seriousness and hard work and not on riding the high horse.

Host

Host in himself — (*one with great skill*). Pandit Nehru was a host in himself.

Hot

To sell like hot cakes — (*to sell very readily*). Our latest book 'Selected Letters' is selling like hot cakes.

To blow hot and cold — (*to contradict oneself*). In today's meeting the speaker was blowing hot and cold.

Hot and hot — (*served as soon as cooked*). The service in Standard Restaurant is worth appreciating; you get things hot and hot.

In hot water — (*in trouble*). The stealing habit of Marshal has brought the whole family in hot water this morning.

Hotch

Hotch-potch — (*mixture*). Let us have something hotch-potch.

Hour

At the eleventh hour — (*at the last moment*). Help reached our army at the eleventh hour.

His hour has come —(*he is about to die*). The old man's hour has come.

House

To keep open house — (*to provide entertainment to all comers*). Any club is supposed to keep an open house.

House to house — (*door to door*). They moved house to house for collecting charity.

Like a house on fire — (*vigorously*). Mohan worked like a house on fire and got first class in his examination.

How

Hows and whys — (*the manner and the cause*). We are unable to follow the hows and whys of your problem.

Hue

Hue and cry — (*a great noise; a loud clamour about something*). The manager could not listen to us as there was hue and cry in the office.

I

Ice

To break the ice — (*to start conversation*). For nearly ten minutes nobody broke the ice in the meeting.

Cut no ice — (*without any effect*). It cuts no ice on me wheather you stay here or go.

Ill

To take ill — (*to mind*). Please don't take ill of what Ramesh has just said.

To be ill at ease — (*to be uneasy*). You will always be ill at ease in an immature company.

To be taken ill — (*to fall ill*). My brother has suddenly taken ill this morning.

In

In brief — (*in short*). Please tell us the whole matter in brief.

Ins and outs — (*full information*). A leader must keep himself informed of ins and outs of latest achievements in the country.

In time — The train left in time.

In pursuance of — (*while doing it*). He is studying science in pursuance of his desire to become a doctor.

In a body — (*together with one feeling*). The decision of appointing Shri Dinesh as a new Secretary was taken at the meeting in a body.

To be in for a thing — (*determined to get a thing done*). He is in for a job now-a-days.

Inch

By inches — (*by small degrees*). Do not hurry, do things by inches.

Every inch — (*entirely*). Every inch of this property belongs to me.

An inch of cold iron — (*stab with a dagger*). The old man lost his wife with an inch of cold iron.

Incumbent

To be incumbent — (*essential*). A general clerk should be incumbent of typing.

Indifference

A matter of indifference — (*unimportant*). Flood havocs in the country can hardly be a matter of indifference to anyone.

Infancy

In infancy — (*in childhood*). He lost his parents in infancy.

Inferiority

Inferiority complex — (*feeling of being inferior*). Inferiority complex does not allow any one to rise in one's life.

Inferno

To let loose an inferno — (*to kill, murder and burn indiscriminately*). During the war many nations let loose and inferno.

Influence

Back-door influence — (*improper approach*). He got the job through back-door influence.

Initiative

To take the initiative — (*to take the lead*). Unless someone takes initiative in the matter it is not going to be solved.

Innate

Innate ideas — (*inborn ideas*). Mahatma Gandhi's innate ideas made him the leader of our country.

Inside

Inside story — (*behind the scene*). No one knows the inside story of this big scandal.

To have the inside track — (*to have the advantageous position*). He has the inside track in his interview.

Instance

At the instances of — (*under the direction of*). At the instance of his uncle he applied for the job and got it.

To give instances — (*to take examples*). Don't explain things by giving instances, just show us something solid.

Intent

To all intents and purposes — (*practically*). To all intents and purposes he is a useless boy.

Interval

At intervals — (*now and then*). He does things at intervals.

Intrude

To intrude upon — (*to interfere with*). Do not intrude upon my work.

Iron

Man of iron — (*of strong mind*). Vallabhbhai Patel was a man of Iron.

Iron will — (*strong mind*). I have an iron will to succeed in my new business.

To strike while the iron is hot — (*to make use of an opportunity in time*). By his applying for this job he struck while the iron was hot.

In irons — (*in fetters*). Every thief finds himself in irons one day or the other.

Issue

Issue of fact — (*when issue is denied*). Your statement is an issue of fact.

At issue — (*under discussion*). At issue is the subject of expansion of education in India.

J

Jack

Jack of all trades — (*one who can do all things*). Ramesh is jack of all trades but master of none.

Black Jack — (*vessel for liquor*). In yesterday's raid, the police recovered 20 black jacks.

Jackal

To act as Jackal — (*to do preparatory work*). The stenographer acts as jackal of the manager.

Jam

Money for jam — (*money for nothing*). Don't waste money for jam.

To jam into — (*to thrust violently into something*). His cycle jammed into a bus and he died on the spot.

Jar

To jar upon — (*to irritate*). Do not jar upon your inferiors.

Ajar — (*open*). The thieves left the box ajar.

To jar with — (*disagree*). On hearing facts, I jarred with your scheme.

Jaw

To Jaw — (*to annoy with words*). The clerk was dismissed because he jawed his manager.

Hold your jaw — (*stop talking*). Will you please hold your jaw and listen to me ?

Jay

Jay-walker — (*who walks on round without paying any heed to traffic rules*). Jay-walking is an easy road to hospital.

Jerry

Jerry shop — (*low beer shop*). The whole town is full of jerry shops.

Jest

In jest — (*not seriously*). A person doing things in jest never succeeds in life.

Jew

Rich as a jew — (*very wealthy*). The old rich Jew of this city expired this morning.

Worth a Jew's eye — (*quite precious*). The ornaments presented by Abdullah are worth a Jew's eye.

Jib

The cut of one's jib — (*personal appearance*). The cut of her jib is very attractive.

Jitterbug

Jitterbug — (*one addicted to dancing*). The taste for jitterbug among young girls is fast spreading in our country.

Job

On the job — (*in action*). When the clerk came in, the peon was working on the job.

Job comforter — (*one who under the guise of comfort aggravates distress*). Ram is a job comforter.

Jockey

To Jockey — (*to pilot; cheat*). It is unfair on his part for having jockeyed his brother in business.

Jog

Jog trot — (*a slow but rugular walk*). The police family is in the habit of having a jog trot in the morning.

Jog away; Jog off — (*get away*). The police ordered the demonstrators to jog away within three minutes.

Join

Join hands — (*to be united*). Let us join hands before starting this new venture.

Join up — (*enlist in the army*). The national emergency necessitates young men of India to join up defence.

Join battle — (*begin fighting*). The country is going to join battle very soon.

Joint

During the joint lives — (*when they are all alive*). The children enjoy their best during the joint lives of their parents.

Out of joint — (*out of order*). My scooter went out of joint this morning.

Joke

No joke — (*a serious matter*). There is no joke in our principal's speech.

Practical joke — (*a harmful joke*). Never play practical jokes on your friends.

Jolly

A jolly dog — (*a jovial fellow*). A jolly dog is liked in every company.

The jolly fool — (*a happy person*). His brother does not like the company of jolly fools.

A jolly good fellow — (*a very social and popular fellow*). Krishan became a jolly good fellow only after joining our club.

Joy

Joy-ride — (*ride in a car for enjoyment*). Joy-rides are very popular in America.

Judas

Judas kiss (*false love*). His wife's love was a judas kiss.

Juggle

To juggle with — (*deceive*). Never juggle with your friends.

Jump

To jump a claim — (*to seize somebody else's claim*). Immediately after the death of his father the eldest son jumped a claim on his younger brother.

To jump up — (*to rise*). His honesty is the main cause of his jumping up to his position.

To jump at an offer — (*to accept its eagerly*). My brother jumped at the offer of Superintendent's post in his office.

To jump upon — (*to attack*). The Chinese jumped upon Indians in 1962.

To jump to — (*to decide quickly*). Our manager is in the habit of jumping to wrong conclusions.

To jump together — (*to agree*). All members jumped together on the secretary's suggestion of constructing new buildings.

Jump down — (*fall*). There is hardly any chance of jumping down the prices of essential commodities.

Justice

To do justice to — (*to treat fairly*). A student should always do full justice to his studies.

Keck

To keck at — (*reject*). I cannot keck at my uncle's offer to join him as manager.

Keen

Keen eye — (*fully alive*). One must have a keen eye to be successful in life.

Keen set — (*hungry*). I don't like people keen set at money.

Keep

Keep your hair on — (*don't lose your temper*). Let us keep our hair on and settle the matter amicably.

Keep open house — (*entertain all comers*). A club must keep open house.

To keep at arm's length — (*to check one from becoming too familiar*). He likes to keep himself at arm's length.

Keep one's balance — (*to remain stable*). It is difficult to keep one's balance due to the high cost of living.

To keep body and soul together — (*to sustain life*). The present unemployment does not offer to keep body and soul together.

Keep house — (*remain indoors*). Many Indians advise their young daughters and sisters to keep house.

To keep down — (*to keep expenses low*). His meagre income compels him to keep down his budget.

To keep in with — (*to maintain friendly relations*). India always tries to keep herself in with other countries.

To keep in touch — (*to remain in contact with*). A pilot has always to keep himself in touch with the nearest airport.

To keep to oneself — (*to refuse to share it*). The amount left with me is so small that I have to keep it to myself.

Keep on — (*continue*). Please keep on with your work.

Keeping with — (*according to*). In keeping with the traditions of his family the boy got married in a royal family.

Out of keeping with — (*not according to*). It is out of keeping with the principles of my life.

Ken

Beyond one's ken — (*out of one's sight*). Beyond one's ken, beyond one's mind.

Kettle

A pretty kettle of fish — (*awkward state of affairs*). A pretty kettle of fish exists in our office.

Key

Key industry — (*key main basic industry*). A country has to subsidise its key industry always.

Golden and silver key — (*money used as bribe*). The habit of golden and silver key must be curtailed in the country.

Keynote — (*main idea*). The keynote of the plan is to provide reasonable shelter to poor people.

Key up — (*stimulate*). Key up your digestion

Key — (*that solves some difficulty*). Poison is not necessarily the only key for a distressed man.

Kick

To kick the bucket — (*to die*). All of us have to kick the bucket one day.

More kicks than half pence — (*more abuse than profit*). The business he has started has more kicks than half pence.

To kick against the pricks — (*to invite trouble*). No wise man will ever kick against the pricks.

To kick up dust or a row — (*to create trouble*). The little kid is kicking up dust for every one.

Kid

To handle with kid gloves — (*to handle with ease*) This matter must be handled with kid gloves.

Kill

A killing pace — (*exhausting*). A mine is always a killing pace.

To kill time — (*to waste time*). Parents must check their children from killing time.

To kill two birds with one stone — (*to serve two purposes simultaneously*). The manager of the company is clever enough to kill two birds with one stone.

Kin

Kith and kin — (*relative*). All his kith and kin were present during the time of his wedding.

Kind

Of a kind — (*the same kind*). We are using tea leaves of a kind being used in good restaurants.

After their kind — (*after their customs*). Many Hindus have blind faith of working after their kind.

In kind — (*payment in goods*). In villages, labourers are paid generally in kind.

King

King of kings — (*God*). Nothing is hidden from the king of kings.

King of terrors — (*death*). A soldier is never afraid of the kings of terrors.

The king of beasts — (*lion*). The king of beasts was let loose in the circus last night.

Kiss

Kiss the dust — (*to humble oneself*). Unless one has the quality of kissing the dust, one cannot rise in life.

To kiss the book — (*to kiss the Bible*). The Father kisses the book in Church.

To kiss one's hand — (*to wish one bon-voyage*). When the train moved the father kissed his daughter's hand.

Kit

The whole kit of them — (*the whole lot of them*). The whole kit of the factory labour is at work.

Kite

To fly a kite — (*to test public opinion*). No Government can fly a kite for long.

Knee

To bring to knees — (*to reduce to submission*). The Guru was able to bring to knees all his new Shishyas.

To give knee to — (*to support*). Please give knee to your youngsters.

Is on the knees of the gods — (*yet uncertain*). The success in examination is still on the knees of the gods.

Knife

To get a knife into — (*to kill*). The thief got a knife into the old man.

Before you can say knife — (*very quickly*). The man is intelligent enough to do his work before you can say knife.

Knock

To knock down — (*strike to the ground*). In the quarrel the old man was knocked down.

To knock about — (*to wander about*). Do not knock about the girls.

To take the knock — (*to hard hit financially*). I am taking the knock now-a-days.

To knock the bottom out of — (*to make an argument ineffective*). In election every leader tries to knock the bottom out of his opponents.

Knock out — (*to defeat*). India knocked out Australia by three wickets.

To knock against — (*to collide*). The car knocked against the tree.

Knock together — (*put hastily together*). The thieves were able to knock together jewellery and clothes.

Know

Know-nothing — (*ignorant person*). I am know-nothing about the murder.

Know-nothingness — (*ignorance*). Your know-nothingness will not solve the problem.

Know-how — (*knowledge of how to do something*). The technical know-how about many foreign machines lacks in India.

In the know of — (*having confidential information*). We are in the know of the company's affairs.

To know one's mind — (*to be able to decide within one's own self*). It is no use talking to a person who doesn't know his mind.

Knowledge

To my knowledge — (*so far as I know*). To the best of my knowledge he is a good boy.

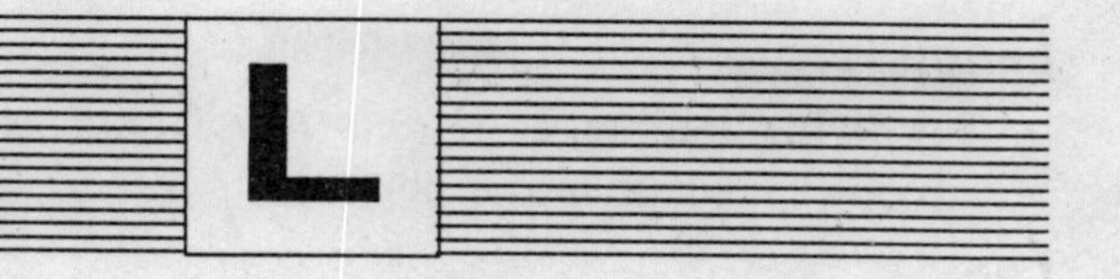

Labour

Labouring heart — (*troubled mind*). A labouring heart cannot do a good job.

At lost labour — (*hard work has resulted in nothing*). All efforts of Rajesh to get through in the examination proved a lost labour.

Herculean labour — (*needing enormous labour*). Any industry needs Herculean labour now-a-days.

Lack

Lack lustre — (*dull*). Science is a lack lustre subject for many.

Lady

Ladies man — (*one who is fond of female society*). Manohar is a ladies man.

Lady of easy virtue — (*a prostitute*). Every big city has professional ladies of easy virtue.

Your good lady — (*your wife*). Your good lady was with my sister last evening.

Lady-love — (*sweetheart*). When he failed in getting his lady-love he committed suicide.

Lamb

A wolf in lamb's clothing — (*hypocrite*). Many sadhus are like wolves in lamb's clothing now-a-days.

Land

Landslide — (*overwhelming majority*). Kripalani got a landslide victory in the last election.

Land of the living — (*present life*). It is difficult to maintain land of the living in our country due to high cost of living.

Land of the leal — (*heaven*). May God the old woman rest in the land of the leal.

Language

A living language — (*one that is still spoken*). English is a living language in our country.

Lap

Lapped in luxury — (*brought up in luxury*). The whole family of my in-laws is lapped in luxury.

Large

At large — (*at liberty*). The thief is at large.

Latter

Latter end — (*death*). The time of latter end has come for the old man.

Laugh

To laugh on the wrong side of the mouth — (*to have revulsion from joy to tears*). Do not laugh on the wrong side of the mouth.

To laugh in one's sleeves — (*to be secretly amused*). The habit of laughing on one's sleeves is good in some cases only.

Laurel

To win laurels — (*to win honours*). One must win laurels in life.

To look to one's laurels — (*to be afraid of losing fame*). A film star always looks to his laurels.

Lavender

To lay lavender — (*to set aside something for future use*). The Government is trying to encourage the habit of laying lavender in our country.

Law

To lay down the law — (*to talk authoritatively*). Unless you are in a position to lay down the law, we are not willing to listen to you.

To take the law into one's own hands — (*to redress one's wrong by force*). During war many nations try to take the law into their own hands.

Be a law to oneself — (*to disregard convention*). Let us not be a law to ourselves.

To give the law to — (*to impose one's will upon*). Giving the law in the hands of immature is no wisdom.

Lay

To lay stress upon — (*to impress*). The teacher laid stress upon the students to work hard for their examination.

To lay out — (*to display*). Our books are being laid out by all the good shopkeepers.

Lay hand on — (*findout*). The Government wants to lay hands on the property of some rich people.

The lazy bones — (*idlers*). You cannot expect good results from the lazy bones.

Lead

To lead one a life — (*worry one constantly*). She leads the whole family a life.

To lead the way — (*to go first*). If the secretary of our union agrees, I shall be glad to lead the way.

To lead astry — (*to misguide*). The tourist was led astry by some bad people who robbed him afterwards.

To lead by the nose — (*make one obey one's orders*). He leads the servant by the nose.

Easier led than driven — (*guide by persuasion*). Even a worker is easier led than driven now-a-days.

Men of light and leading — (*of great influence*). All the members of the Labour Party in London are men of light and leading.

Leaf

To turn over a new leaf — (*to start afresh*). After the marriage he turned over a new leaf in his life.

To take a leaf out of one's book — (*to do as one does*). Let us all take a leaf out of Nehru's book.

Lean

Lean year — (*famine*). A lean year is generally followed after the war.

Leap

A leap in the dark — (*an action undertaken without judging its results*). No wise man will ever leap in the dark.

By leaps and bounds — (*very quickly*). The whole country is progressing by leaps and bounds.

Leave

To take leave of one's senses — (*to go mad*). In anger he murdered his wife and then took leave of his senses.

Lee

To make up leeway — (*to struggle out of bad position*). At last my brother was able to make up leeway.

Leeward — (*with the winds*). Let us move with leeward.

There are lees to every wine — (*even the best article have some defects*).

Left

Over the left — (*a negative*). The whole job has been done over the left.

Leg

On his legs — (*making a speech*). The professor collapsed while on his legs.

Shake a leg — (*dance*). A person who does not know how to shake his legs is not fit for joining a club.

To pull one's legs — (*to deceive*). Never pull legs of your friends.

Without a leg to stand on — (*with no support*). Without a leg to stand on one cannot win elections.

On one's last legs — (*near death*). The old man is on his last legs.

Leisure

At leisure — (*not occupied*). The time is so hard that we cannot afford to be at leisure these days.

Lend

To lend an ear — (*to hear*). Will you please lend me your ear ?

Let

To let down — (*to bring down*). My friends tried to let me down in time of need.

Let off — (*to allow to go free without punishment*). The thief was let off by the police after they were bribed.

Let is be — (*do not interfere with*). Let it be as it is.

Letter

Man of letters — (*a literary person*). The writer of this book is a man of letters.

To the letter — (*with adherene to every detail*). The company has accepted the manager's proposal to the letter.

In letter and spirit — (*in form and in substance*). The Tashkent Agreement has been observed in the letter and spirit.

Letter perfecting — (*knowing one's part perfectly*). One should always be letter perfect in one's job.

Level

Level-headed — (*clever*). Be careful of that level-headed man.

Do one's level best — (*to exert to the maximum*). I did my level best in the exams, but unfortunately I failed.

On level with — (*equal with*). In sports both the brothers are on level with one another.

Lick

Lick the dust — (*to die*). Just a few minutes after the accident, the dog licked the dust.

To lick into shape — (*to give a nice appearance*). The young girl is licking into shape.

Lickpenny — (*that which makes the money go*). Life in any big city is lickpenny now-a-days.

Lid

With the lid off — (*with all its horrors*). I witnessed many deaths with the lid off during the partition.

Lie

To give the lie to — (*to contradict a false statement*). The Manager has given the lie to what his P.A. was saying regarding his promotion.

To act a lie — (*to deceive*). Do not act a lie with your friends.

To lie over — (*to be postponed*). The board's meeting has been laid over for tomorrow.

To give one the lie — (*to prove one to be wrong*). The student gave professor the lie.

Let sleeping dogs lie — (*avoid debatable questions*). Be wise always and let sleeping dogs lie.

Lieu

In lieu of — (*instead of*). In lieu of his going, I shall myself go there and see what can be done.

Life

To lay down one's life — (*to sacrifice one's life*). Many Indians laid down their lives for the freedom of the country.

To bring to life — (*to revive*). Bring to life the old file.

A matter of life and death — (*very critical*). It is a matter of life and death for me to seek any job at this age.

Escape with life and limb — (*escape completely*). Even during such a critical stage he escaped with life and limb.

For life — (*as long as I live*). I am devoted to this cause for life.

Light

To light upon — (*to find by accident*). Only lucky people light upon success.

To bring to light — (*expose*). By his arrest many things have been brought to light.

Throw light upon — (*explain*). Will you please throw more light upon your suggestions ?

light come light go — (*a thing which is easily acquired is easily lost*). Money earned in this way is always light come light go.

Limb

Limb of the devil — (*a mischievous child*). Pinky is a limb of the devil.

Limb of the law — (*one who deals with the law*). Limbs of the law must do justice with their duties.

Line

Line upon line — (*little by little*). They are doing the work line upon line.

To read between the line — (*to catch the secret meaning*). I can easily read between the lines of his statement.

Linen

To wash dirty linen in public — (*to abuse one another publicly*). It is always wise to avoid washing the dirty linen in public.

Lion

Lion's share — (*the larger part*). The managing partner has the lion's share in the company's profit.

Lion in the way — (*obstacles*). There are many lions in the way for me for getting a suitable job.

To place one's head in the lions mouth — (*to expose oneself unnecessarily to a danger*). During the partition many people placed their heads in the lion's mouth to save their kith and kin.

Lip

To bite one's lips — (*to express annoyance*). When the student was not able to solve the problem inspite of the teacher's explaining thrice the teacher bit his lips.

To hang one's lips — (*to be in humiliation*). There is no harm in hanging one's lips sometimes.

To curl the lip — (*to express contempt*). Suneeta curled her lips while glancing at that scoundrel.

Live

To live from hand to mouth — (*to live miserably*). With this meagre amount they have to live from hand to mouth.

Loaf

Loaves and fishes — (*personal profits*). Every man now-a-days tries to make for his loaves and fishes.

Loin

To grid up one's loins — (*to prepare for the effort*). He has completed his studies and is now griding up his loins for a job.

Long

To long and the short — (*in brief*). Please tell me the whole story in the long and the short.

Long-headed — (*clever*). The long-headed peon deceived his employer.

To draw the long bow — (*to exaggerate*). Do not draw the long bow of your income, otherwise income-tax people will trouble you.

Look

To look up to — (*respect*). The students should always look up to their teachers.

To look black — (*to be black with anger*). The father looked black on his drunkard son.

Look through — (*study*). Look through hard and get good marks in your examination.

To look down upon — (*to hate*). The stage has come when he will look down upon his wife.

Loose

At a loose end — (*without employment*). My brother is at the loose end for the last three months.

Living on the loose — (*to lead an immoral life*). Many young girls who are kidnapped are forced to live on the loose.

With a loose rein — (*indulgently*). She lives with a loose rein.

Loss

To be at a loss — (*unable to decide*). I am at a loss to understand what you are saying.

Lose

Losing game — (*in which defeat is certain*). Life is a losing game for every rich and poor.

To lose patience — (*to become restless*). Never lose patience if you want to rise in life.

To lose cold — (*get rid of*). Let us try to lose cold from the bad company.

Lot

Bad lot — (*a disreputable person*). The manager of the company has become a bad lot now.

Lottery

Lottery — (*chance prize*). He won the Derby Lottery last year.

Lotus

Lotus eating — (*indolent enjoyment*). Are you fond of lotus eating ?

Love

For the love of — (*for the sake of*). For the love of his job he lost everything.

Not for love or money — (*unobtainable*). You may do your best but it is not for love or money.

In love with — (*enamoured*). She is in love with Suraj.

Low

In low waters — (*out of funds*). The club is in low waters these days.

To lay low — (*to kill*). He tried to lay low his friend but was caught at the spot.

Luck

Down on one's luck — (*short of money and chances*). The whole family of my friend is down on their luck now-a-days.

Not in luck's way — (*in the normal way*). The circumstances are not in luck's way for me.

He has the luck of the devil — (*everything that he touches turns into gold*).

Lump

In the lump — (*wholesale*). We are interested in buying this in the lump.

Lump sum — (*in one sum*). Please make payment of my bills in lump sum.

A lump of selfishness — (*selfish through and through*). The man with a lump of selfishness is never successful in life.

Lurch

To leave in the lurch — (*to desert*). Please do not go abroad otherwise your family will be left in the lurch.

Mail

Mailed fist — (*military might*). India has to raise her mailed fist during the National Emergency.

Main

Mainstay — (*main support*). The mainstay for the patient is his regular medicine.

To splice the mainbrace — (*to indulge freely in strong drinks*). Many young Indians splice the main-brace now-a-days.

Majority

To attain majority — (*to come of age*). My son has attained the age of majority only yesterday.

To join the majority — (*to die*). The old fellow has joined the majority last night.

Make

To make off — (*to run away*). The thief made off with the car.

To make or mar — (*to cause success or ruin*). The labour of a man makes or mars his career.

To make good — (*to fulfil one's promise*). He will make good the whole loss.

To make free with — (*to take liberties with*). That girl is trying to make free with everybody.

To make after — (*to pursue*). Please make after this matter when I go out.

To make away with — (*to kill*). He shot to make away with the manager but missed it.

Make out — (*understand*). I cannot make out head or tail of your statement.

On the make — (*looking after personal benefits*). My friend is on the make now-a-days.

Malt

In meal or malt — (*in one way or the other*). I want to settle it in meal or malt.

Man

Man is the moon — (*very rare person*). You have become a man in the moon now-a-days.

Man of letters — (*a literary scholar*). There is still great dearth of men of letters in our country.

Man of straw — (*good for nothing*). There is no use keeping the company of men of straw.

Man in the street — (*common man*). Men in the street are the worst sufferers in war.

Many

Many men, many winds — (*as many opinions as there are persons to give them*). Many men, many minds never make a meeting successful.

Map

Off the map — (*of no account*). Sudershan is now off the map of office.

March

To steal a march — (*to surpass*). My brother stole a march over all his colleagues.

Mark

A man of mark — (*a notable or famous person*). The late principal of our college was a man of mark.

Upto the mark — (*up to the standard*). The new clerk is just up to the mark.

Beside the mark — (*not to the point*). Please do not talk which is beside the mark.

To hit the mark — (*to achieve one's purpose*). He will hit the mark by hook or by crook.

Below the mark — (*below standard*). The new clerk is below the mark.

Market

To come to the market — (*to be offered for sale*). The grapes have come to the market now-a-days.

To bring one's hog to a bad market — (*fall in prices*). The fruit sellers were able to bring their hogs to a bad market.

Mass

In the mass — (*in general*). The people in the mass are not very intelligent.

The masses — (*the common people*). The masses in our country are ignorant of political implications.

Master

A mastermind — (*expert*). My brother is a mastermind in salesmanship.

Be master of — (*to havè control over*). Always be a master of your children.

Meal

To make meal of — (*consume*). The city has made a meal of the whole available sugar.

Means

by fair or foul means — (*anyhow*). He will get the job done by fair or foul means.

Measure

In a measure — (*to some extent*). In a measure the story seems true.

Beyond measures — (*limitless*). The depth of the sea is beyond measure.

To use hard measure — (*to apply harsh treatment*). The child ran away from the home because his parents were using hard measures against him.

Meet

Meet the case — (*be adequate*). Milk in the utensil will meet the case of whole family.

Meet the eye — (*visible*). When the train left I could meet the eye of my friends for three minutes.

Meet the ear — (*to be audible*). Her voice is so poor that it does not even meet the ear.

Mend

Mend or end — (*improve or finish*). One must mend or end one's life.

Mercy

At the mercy of — (*Wholly in the power of*). The whole world lies at the mercy of God.

Merit

To make a merit of — (*to look the better side of*). A wise man will always try to make a merit of everything.

Merry

Merry Andrew — (*joker*). The last Merry Andrew of the circus performed wonderfully.

To make merry — (*to be jovial*). The Christians make merry on the 'New Year Day'.

Mess

To get into a mess — (*to make things difficult*). His way of work is such that everything in the office gets into mess.

To make a mess of — (*to mismanage*). Please do not make a mess of everything.

Milk

Milk-sop — (*spiritless youth*). Many Asian countries are still full of milk-sops.

To cry over the split milk — (*uselessly bewailing over the damage done*). No use crying over the split milk; it is high time that you should do something.

Milk of human kindness — (*natural kindness*). Only a few are gifted with the milk of human kindness.

Milk and water — (*without energy*). Your working of milk and water will be of no material help to you.

Mill

To see through a mill-stone — (*to see through difficult questions*). The whole class is seeing through a mill-stone in the examinations.

To put through the mill — (*to give training*). Universities in India are planning to put through the mill all the students so that they are successful in the professions.

To go through the mill — (*to go through suffering*). His family is going through the mill now-a-days.

Mincemeat

To make mincemeat of — (*to destroy*). In war every soldier wants to make a mincemeat of the opponent.

Mind

To call to mind — (*to remember*). I don't call to mind having told you that I will give you a job.

Mind your own business — (*not to interfere in other's affairs*). Will you please mind your own business ?

Of one mind — (*agreed*). The whole college was of one mind except the principal.

Make up one's mind — (*determine*). Please make up your mind and appear in the examination.

Half a mind — (*hesitant*). Never go for an interview with half a mind.

Mistake

Mistaken kindness — (*harmful help*). I don't want your mistaken kindness.

And no mistake — (*without fail*). He will come there and no mistake.

Mister

Be he prince or mere mister — (*everybody*). Be he prince or mere mister, one must die.

Mite

Not a mite — (*not at all*). The child had not a mite of milk.

A mite of a child — (*very small child*). He is a mite of a child for going to school at this stage.

Mix

To be mixed up — (*involved*). Let us not be mixed up in others affairs.

Mix up with — (*thoroughly confused*). Please do not mix up with office accounts or else you will be in trouble one day.

Mixed school — (*co-educational school*). Mixed schools are increasing in every backward country these days.

Mole

To make a mountain of a molehill — (*to exaggerate*). It is not wise on your part to make a mountain of a molehill of your family affairs.

Moment

Man of moment — (*important person*). Nehru was a man of moment.

Of great moment — (*of great importance*). Kashmir is a matter of great moment for both India and Pakistan.

Money

Pots of money — (*a large number of money*). Pots of money are required to start any business.

Money for jam — (*profitable return for labour*). Investment in stocks and shares is money for jam.

For love or money — (*anyhow*). Everyone must try to succeed in life for love or money.

Money's worth — (*worth of money*). Investment in our business is money's worth.

Monkey

monkey tricks — (*deceitful action*). His monkey tricks brought the whole family into trouble.

Young monkey — (*playful*). A boy is a young monkey.

Moon

Once in a blue moon — (*seldom*). Your visits to our place are once a blue moon.

Minions of the moon — (*thieves who rob by night*). Minions of the moon were able to run away with five thousand rupees, last night.

It is all moonshine — (*it is nonsense*). Will you please stop your moonshine?

Moonshine — (*visionary*). Moonshine plans are never successful.

Mop

Mop the floor with — (*have overwhelming advantage*). The principal was able to mop the floor with his speech.

More

To be no more — (*dead*). Her father is no more in the world.

More or less — (*approximately*). The cloth he purchased is more or less for one shirt.

Mortal

Mortal agony — (*death*). Mortal agony is knocking the door of the patient.

Mortal hurry — (*in great hurry*). Please give me a ticket. I am in mortal hurry to see the beginning of the film.

Moss

A Rolling stone gathers no moss — (*One who is constantly changing his profession*) A rolling stone is never successful in life).

Mother

Every mother's son — (*everybody*). Every mother's son in this meeting must listen to me.

Mother wit — (*common sense*). Mother wit lacks in many young people.

Mother tongue — (*one's native tongue*). His mother tongue is Spanish.

Mother earth — (*earth as mother of its inhabitants*). We must worship the mother earth.

Motion

To put in motion — (*to set moving*). Put in motion the machine and let us see how it works.

In motion — (*moving*). Do not get down from the bus while it is in motion.

Mouth

Mouth waters — (*tempts*). His mouth waters at the sight of sweets.

Hold your mouth — (*hold your tongue*). Will you please hold your mouth and listen to us now ?

Put words in his mouth — (*tell him what to say*). Please put some words in your brother's mouth.

Move

Make a move — (*to go*). Will you please make a move from here now ?

To move heaven and earth — (*to make strenuous efforts*). The boy moved heaven and earth but he failed in the examination.

On the move — (*in motion*). The train is on the move.

Mud

To throw mud at — (*to make unworthy charges*). Those who stay in mud houses should not throw mud on others.

Muddle

Muddle through — (*attain one's end*). Somehow or the other he is always able to muddle through his work.

Muddle on — (*get on in a haphazard way*). It is high time that you should improve and leave the habit of muddling on with your work.

Music

Rough music — (*noisy uproar*). The children are making rough music in the school.

To face the music — (*to face the consequence*). Stop your habit of cheating or else you have to face its music one day.

Mustard

Mustard plaster — (*zestful person*). Mustard plasters are always successful in life.

Grain of mustard seed — (*small thing capable of vast development*). Agriculture is fast becoming a grain of mustard seed.

Mutton

Dead as mutton — (*absolutely dead*). The topic is now as dead as mutton.

Nail

On the nail — (*at once*). I cannot give you any money on the nail.

Hard as nails — (*in fine training*). Soldiers are hard as nails.

Nail up — (*close*). The matter is nailed up once for all.

To nail to the counter — (*to expose a falsehood*). Unless you nail to the counter, nobody will know the truth.

Naked

Stark naked — (*entirely naked*). When he returned home he found his wife stark naked.

The naked truth — (*truth without trimming*). The naked truth is before you.

In its naked absurdity — (*undisguised*). One could see the truth in its naked absurdity.

Name

In the name of — (*by the authority of*). In the name of the Prime Minister, many people are collecting donations.

To call names — (*to abuse*). He is in the habit of calling names to every one.

To name the day — (*to fix the day of the wedding*). Her mother had come to name the day for Sarla.

To put one's name down for — (*to apply as a candidate*). Manoj has also put his name down for the post of a clerk.

Nap

To catch on napping — (*to come upon when one is unprepared*). Chinese caught Indians napping in 1962.

Nap hand — (*taking risk for something success of which is almost certain*). 'Lucky' horse has a nap hand on the racing bets.

Narrow

Narrow escape — (*to escape with the slightest margin*). He had a narrow escape.

Narrow-minded — (*mean*). Narrow-minded people are never successful in life.

Within narrow bounds — (*in limit*). I am within narrow bounds of my financial circumstances.

Narrow circumstances — (*poverty*). He is passing through narrow circumstances now-a-days.

Nature

By nature — (*inherently*). He speaks the truth by nature.

In nature — (*existing everywhere*). Love is in nature.

In a state of nature — (*nude or naked*). When I returned home, I found the child in a state of nature.

Naught

To come to naught — (*to come to nothing*). Unless you work hard, your first class plans will come to naught.

To set at naught — (*to treat as of no account*). His brother set at naught all his feelings.

Nay

Will not take nay — (*disregards; refusals*). He will not take nay.

Cannot say one nay — (*cannot contradict one*). Unless he has guts he cannot say nay to you.

Near

Far and near — (*everywhere*). People come in the fair from far and near.

Nearby — (*close by*). His house is nearby to that school.

Nearest to one's heart — (*dear*). Sumedha is nearest to my heart.

Necessity

Of necessity — (*unavoidable*). With these finances at my disposal I can only go in for things of necessity.

Necessity knows no law — (*when a thing is necessarily required in a country, it has to make a virtue of necessity*).

To make a virtue of necessity —(*to laugh through what is inevitable*). He always tries to make a virtue of necessity.

Neck

Neck and crop — (*completely*). The floods have destroyed the village neck and crop.

Neck and neck — (*side by side*). Let us walk neck and neck.

To save one's neck — (*to escape punishment*). The thief cannot save his neck.

To get it upto the neck — (*to be completely defeated*). Once Pakistan starts war it will get it upto the neck from India.

Needle

To hit the needle — (*to make a perfect hit*). Unless you hit the needle in getting a job Suneeta's father is not going to marry her to you.

The needle — (*fit of nervousness*). He suffered the needle.

Negative

Negative causes of dissatisfaction — (*signs of omission*). Negative causes of dissatisfaction are really worse.

Nerve

A fit of nerves — (*a nervous state*). Many soldiers suffer a fit of nerves in war.

To posses nerves of steel — (*to be unperturable*). Great men possess nerves of steel.

To get on one's nerves — (*to worry*). One should never get on one's nerves.

Nest

Nest egg — (*money laid by*). A wise business man always maintains a nest egg.

Hornet's nest — (*dangerous place*). Few take the courage of going to hornet's nest.

To feather one's own nest — (*to enrich oneself at the cost of others*). Many ministers are feathering their own nest now-a-days.

Nether

Nether world — (*hell*). He is living in a nether world now-a-days.

Never

Better late than never — (*it is better to do something good however late, than not to do it at all*). Start with your studies right now; it is better late than never.

It is never too late to mend — (*one can improve matters at any stage*). Pandit Nehru had the quality of doing anything at the stage when it was never too late to mend.

New

New fangled — (*newly achieved*). New-fangled things do not last long.

To turn over a new leaf — (*to lead a new life*). After marriage, every person has to turn over a new leaf.

Next

Next to nothing — (*almost nothing at all*). His arguments command a respect which is next to nothing.

Next of kin — (*nearest relative*). He is next of my kin.

Next door — (*in the neighbourhood*). She stays next door to me.

Nick

In the nick of time — (*just at the right moment*). I reached the station in the nick of time of leaving the train.

To nick the nick — (*to win or accomplish*). He nicked the nick by getting first prize in the examination.

Niddle-noddle

Niddle-noddle — (*unsteady*). His business is niddle-noddle now-a-days.

Nigger

Nigger in the woodpile — (*something that spoils a good thing*). The thoughts of our principal have always niggered in the woodpile.

Night

Day and night — (*at all hours*). Many chemists remain open day and night.

Night-mare — (*dreadful scene*). When I am reminded of the partition of our country. I find a nightmare before me.

night of ignorance — (*barbarous times*). Many countries of the world are still under the night of ignorance.

Nine

Nine times out of ten — (*chances are far greater*). Nine times out of ten, my son is going to get a job in a government office.

Ninth

Ninth part of man — (*tailor*). Your brother is at the shop of a ninth part of a man.

Nip

Nip in the bud — (*to check growth of*). The cholera was nipped in the bud.

Just a nip — (*little wine or beer*). Let us just have a nip.

Nod

On the nod — (*on credit*). I never buy things on the nod.

Land of nod — (*Sleep*). The child has gone to the land of nod.

Nodding acquaintance — (*very slight familiarity*). We have only a nodding acquaintance between us.

Nom de plume

Non de plume — (*writer's borrowed name*). My nom de plume is 'Razia'.

Nose

To count noses — (*to count supporters*). In elections every candidate is confined to counting noses.

Keep nose to the grindstone — (*to face responsibility*). Unless you keep nose to the grindstone your parents will not love you.

To turn up one's nose — (*to express contempt*). I have to turn up my nose from a mean fellow like you.

Plain as the nose in your face — (*easily seen*). His face is plain as the nose in the face.

Notable

A notable quantity — (*perceptible*). A notable quantity of milk is lying at home.

Note

To make a note of — (*to record*). Make a note of this letter.

Nothing

To make nothing of — (*to fail to understand*). We could make nothing of the lecture given by the leader.

To have nothing — (*to be without individuality*). We have nothing with us.

Come to nothing — (*turn out useless*). Many an Indian plan comes to nothing.

To be nothing — (*to be untrue*). I find nothing in his statement.

Notice

To come into notice — (*to attract attention*). She was the cause of coming into notice.

Nowhere

Nowhere near — (*not nearby*). Nowhere near is plenty of water in Rajasthan.

Nut

Hard nut to crack — (*difficult to convince*). My boss is a hard nut to crack.

O

O.K.

O.K. — (*all correct*). Everything is O.K. with me.

Oar

To pull a good oar — (*to be a good man*). You should pull a good oar.

To put your oar into my boat — (*to unnecessarily interfere in my affairs*). Please do not put your oar into my boat.

Rest on one's oar — (*cease to work jor a time*). The Communist Party of India is resting on its oars.

Oath

To take an oath — (*to swear*). The new Prime Minister has taken an oath to serve the country faithfully.

Observe

The observed of all observers — (*person on whom all attention is concentrated*). The Queen was the observed of all observers during her visit in America.

Occasion

To take occasion — (*to take advantage of an opportunity*). One who takes occasion is always successful in his life.

To take occasion by the forelock — (*to make an immediate use of an opportunity*). Hadn't he taken occasion by the forelock, he wouldn't have been abroad now.

Occupation

Army of occupation — (*army life in a country to hold the occupied region till a regular government is set up*). Russia had an army of occupation.

To occupy oneself with — (*to keep oneself busy*). He is occupying himself with painting.

Ocular

Ocular demonstration — (*proof appearing to the eyes*). Some people are always interested in having an ocular demonstration.

Odd

Odd and ends — (*miscellaneous things*). The beggar was taking odds and ends.

Odd means — (*wrong means*). I do not want to earn any money by odd means.

Odd and even — (*game of chance*). In odd and even he won five thousand rupees.

Take odds — (*accept the advantage*). I want to take odds of going to London.

By long odds — (*by a great difference*). Mohinder got distinction by long odds.

Off

Off and on — (*now and then*). He comes to see me off and on.

Well off — (*in good circumstances*). He is well of now-a-days.

Office

Good offices — (*use for a third party in a dispute*). We have requested his father to use his good offices in settling the dispute between Bhim brothers.

Ill-office — (*disservice*). Avoid ill-office habit.

Oil

To pour oil on the waters — (*smooth matters over*). Only a few leaders can pour oil on the international waters.

Smell of oil — (*bears marks of study*). Krishna's last story published in the paper smells of oil.

Oil the wheels — (*make things go smoothly by courtesy*). For success in life learn the art of oiling the wheels.

Oils one's hand — (*to bribe*). Even oiling one's hand is common at the higher government level.

Old

Old and young — (*everybody*). Old and young of India are going to contribute something towards the Pandit Nehru Memorial Fund.

Old head on young shoulders — (*wisdom beyond years*). Don't try to have your old head on young shoulders.

Old man's beard — (*a kind of moss*). You can't find anything here except old man's beard.

Olive

Olive branches — (*a home for children in relation to their parents*). The feast was attended by Suresh, his wife and their olive branches.

To hold out the olive branch — (*to make overture for peace*). It was after a long war that the Americans were able to hold out the olive branch.

Omnibus

An omnibus bill — (*a bill covering various aspects of questions*). The Sales Tax Bill introduced in parliament was an omnibus bill in the beginning.

On

On and on — (*quickly without stopping*). I read that novel on and on.

On dit — (*rumour*). It is merely an on dit that banks in India will be nationalised soon.

Once

Once for all — (*finally*). Let us close the topic once for all.

Once and again — (*more than once*). Unless you remind him once and again, he will forget to recommend your name.

Once in a way — (*very rarely*). He comes to me once in a way.

Oner

A oner at — (*expert in*). He is a oner at driving.

Only

Only and lonely — (*only*). Rashmi is my only and lonely daughter.

Open

Open heart — (*frankness*). Will you please open your heart ?

Open secret — (*a secret which is no more a secret now*). It is an open secret that he is not going to be appointed to any important positions in the Government now.

Keep open doors — (*be hospitable*). Flt. Lt. Malhotra's whole family keeps open doors.

Open mind — (*an unprejudiced mind*). He has got an open mind.

Operate

To operate — (*to affect*). Try your best, your plans are not going to operate on me.

Operation

To come into operation — (*to become effective*). The medicine given by the doctor is coming into operation now.

Combined operation — (*an army campaign in which land, air and naval forces jointly participate*). War is a combined operation.

Opinion

To act upon one's opinion — (*to put into practice someone's advise*). He always acts upon his father's opinion.

Opposition

Opposition of the thumb — (*persistent opposition*). Every candidate has to face opposition of the thumb in elections.

Option

To have an option — (*to have a choice*). You have an option to stay here or go.

Order

In order — (*Kept/arranged properly*). Everything is lying in order.

Out of order — (*improper*). The car is out of order.

To take order — (*to obey*). The captain took orders from the general.

Of high order — (*of great quality*). The fruits purchased by the event are of high order.

Of low order — (*of low quality*). The books purchased by the boys are of low order.

To order one's life — (*to discipline oneself*). Satish has ordered his life beautifully.

Ostrich

Ostrich belief — (*wrong belief*). He has an ostrich belief in luck.

Have the digestion of an ostrich — (*strong stomach*). I have the digestion of an ostrich.

Other

One or the other — (*anyone out of the two*). Here are two books, you can have one or the other.

The other day — (*some time back*). The other day Professor Jhamb met me and told me that he was going to London.

Oust

Oust from — (*turn out*). The captain has been ousted from the club.

Out

Out and out — (*completely*). He is out and out involved in debts now-a-days.

To be out — (*on strike*). The staff of Mohindra Co. is out today.

Out for — (*out to be*). His financial circumstances compelled him to be out for his misbehaviour.

Outed — (*expelled*). The principal outed Ramzan from college on account of his misbehaviour.

Over

Over and over again — (*very many times*). Practice over and over again makes a man perfect.

Over and above — (*besides*). She purchased a cotton saree over and above a silk saree.

All over — (*finished/dead*). It's all over now.

Owing

Owing one a grudge — (*cherish resentment against*). No use owing a grudge now.

Ox

Black ox — (*misfortune*). Black ox has spoiled his whole career.

An ox in one's tongue — (*bribed to keep mum*). He has been given an ox in his tongue on Kamla's affairs.

P's

To mind one's p's and q's — (*to be accurate and precise*). Mind your p's and q's in your statement.

Pace

To keep pace — (*advance at equal speed*). Keep pace with time.

To put a person through his paces — (*to test qualities of a person, in action*). If you don't believe me, you can put him through his paces.

Pack

Pack off — (*to send off quickly*). Pack of your dishonest peon.

A pack of fools — (*a group of idiots*). Yamin comes from the company of a pack of fools.

To pack up — (*to go out of action*). The cycle is packed up.

Pad

Stand-pad — (*to beg by the roadside*). I found him stand-pad.

Page

Page of honour — (*officer of the royal house*). The President of Yugoslavia has many pages of honour.

To fill a page in history — (*to be remembered in history*). The life of Nehru will fill a page in history.

Pains

To take pains — (*to work hard*). If you take pains in your work, you will surely succeed.

Under pains of — (*subject to penalty of*). I have to go to my office even during this sickness under pains of losing the job.

To be at the pains of — (*doing*). He is at the pains of writing an essay.

Paint

To paint the town red — (*to enjoy very much*). When he got first class all his family members painted the town red.

To paint one black — (*to criticise a person malignantly*). Many a sadhu is the subject of painting them black now-a-days.

Painted lady — (*a butterfly*). A painted lady is sitting on the floor.

Pair

Pair of colours — (*two flags carried by a regiment, the national flag as also the regimental colour*). The battalion is marching with a pair of colours in their hand.

Pale

Pale-hearted — (*dispirited*). After failing to get a job for two years, he has now become pale-hearted.

To look pale before — (*to be nothing as compared with*). Renu looks pale before Usha.

Palm

To grease a person's palm — (*to bribe*). It is difficult to see an officer without greasing the palm of his peon.

Palmy days — (*prosperous days*). Palmy days do come in everyone's life.

Paper

On paper — (*in writing*). Please put your arguments on paper.

Papery plan — (*a plan on paper only*). Many Indian plans are papery plans only.

Paper profits — (*hypothetical gains*). The profits shown by the company are merely paper profits.

Paradise

Fool's paradise — (*foolish ideas*). I don't agree with you, you simply live in a fool's paradise.

Paradise on earth — (*a living heaven*). The rich family of our village is living in a paradise on earth.

Parallel

To draw a parallel — (*to compare*). One cannot draw a parallel between those two friends.

Paramount

On paramount importance — (*very important*). A child is always of paramount importance to his parents.

Part

To take part in (*to share*). I will take part in the next debate.

Part and parcel — (*essential*). Food is part and parcel of one's life.

To part with — (*to separate*). Can you part with your pen for a few hours ?

Particular

In particular — (*specially*). He pointed out Sohan's statement in particular.

Party

Party-spirited — (*with zeal for the party*). Many members of our club are party-spirited.

Pass

To pass away — (*to die*). Pandit Nehru passed away on 27th May 1964.

The pass by — (*to pass by the side of*). I was passing by the Panwalla's shop when I met them last night.

Pass for — (*accepted*). The bill is passed for Rs. 400.

To pass one's lips — (*to reveal a secret*). You can trust Ram, not a word will pass from his lips.

To pass over — (*to omit*). The stenographer passed over the latter portion of Nehru's speech.

Come to pass — (*to happen*). Since his return from abroad many things have come to pass.

Passage

Passage of arms — (*quarrel of words*). A passage of arms is very common in every Parliament.

Passive

Passive resistance — (*to resist non-violently*). A fighter of truth must offer passive resistance to social evils.

Past

A past-master — (*an expert*). He is a past-master in repairing radios.

Pat

To give a pat on the back — (*to give a word of encouragement*). When Babloo informed his father that he got first position in the school, his father gave him a pat on the back.

Patch

To patch up a quarrel — (*to arrange a compromise*). A good mediator can always patch up a quarrel.

Not a patch — (*cannot be compared*). His intelligence is not a patch on his father's.

Patience

Have no patience with — (*irritated*). I have no patience with your silly argument.

Patient

Patient of — (*eager*). The manager is patient of bringing a settlement to the dispute of workers.

Pavement

Crazy pavement — (*irregular*). The old cities in India are still full of crazy pavements.

Pay

To pay off — (*to pay in full*). My employers have paid off my arrears.

In the pay of — (*hired by*). The typewriter is in the pay of the American Ambassador.

To pay one back in one's own coin (*tit for tat*). The attitude of paying one back in one's own coin not always good.

To pay for one's whistle — (*to be punished for one's deeds*). All human beings are paid for their whistles.

Pay down — (*to pay in ready money*). I have yet to pay down for my new scooter.

Peace

Peace at all costs — (*to pay heavy price for peace*). A wise nation will keep peace at all costs but will fight when necessary.

To keep the peace — (*to remain silent*). Will you please keep the peace in the class ?

Pedestal

To put on the pedestal — (*to worship*). Pandit Nehru has been put on the pedestal.

Peg

To peg out — (*to die*). The low temperature will peg out the patient soon.

Off the peg — (*readymade*). I want to buy some goods off the peg.

To take down a peg — (*to humble*). His harsh behaviour has gone and he is now taking down a peg.

Pelt

To pelt one with roses — (*honour one*). The prime Minister was pelted with roses.

Pen

Pen and ink — (*in writing*). Unless you give me your statement in pen and ink I cannot take any action.

Penny

Penny wise pound foolish — (*to get a low cost thing at the cost of very costly thing*).

A penny for your thoughts — (*your thoughts are worthless*). Here's penny for your thoughts.

A pretty penny — (*a good sum of money*). Without a pretty penny it is difficult to manage now-a-days.

Turn an honest penny — (*to earn money honestly*). My father turned an honest penny throughout his life.

Perch

Hop the perch — (*die*). The child has hopped the perch.

Peril

At your peril — (*at your risk*). I am informing you again, all you are doing at your peril.

In peril — (*in danger of*). In peril of his life, the fireman went up to save the child.

Pester

To pester with — (*trouble*). He is pestered with family affairs.

Peter

To peter out — (*to give out*). The whole problem is petering out soon.

Petticoat

Petticoat government — (*predominance of women in the home or politics*). Petticoat governments are rarely successful.

In petticoat — (*small child*). Papu and Rashmi have played together since they were in petticoats.

Phrase

Enough of phrases — (*mere words*). I have enough of phrases from you, will you please give something practicable ?

In simple phrase — (*in simple expression*). Always try to put your ideas in simple phrases.

Physic

A dose of physic — (*medicine*). A dose of physic will cure the child.

Physical

Physical impossibilities — (*absolutely impossible*). The economic theory introduced by Dev is a physical impossibility.

Physical explanation — (*tangible proof*). I want to have a physical explanation of your statement.

Pick

To pick holes in — (*to criticize*). Do not pick holes in other's affairs.

To pick one's pocket — (*to steal from one's pocket*). The thief made an unsuccessful attempt to pick my pocket.

To pick a quarrel — (*to seek fight*). Avoid picking a quarrel with any one.

Pick and choose — (*select fastidiously*). Our manager is an expert at picking and choosing the right man for the right job.

Pick of — (*to choicest*). Meena Kumari was the pick of the Indian film industry.

Pickle

To have a rod in pickle — (*to have a punishment ready*). When the child returned home, his parents were having a rod in pickle.

Picture

The very picture — (*perfect*). The patient looks the very picture of health now.

In the picture — (*one having knowledge of affairs*). So far as office scandal is concerned, the manager is also in the picture.

Piece

All a piece — (*all of the same kind*). So far as intelligence is concerned all the boys of our class are all a piece.

Piece by piece — (*little by little*). I don't mind if you do things piece by piece but please do it right.

Pig

Pig-headed — (*stupid*). Do not talk to that man; he is simply pig-headed.

Pigs might fly — (*wonders might happen*). He can get through only if some pigs fly.

To buy a pig in the poke — (*to buy something without seeing it*). A wise man will never buy a pig in the poke.

Pigeon

Pigeon English — (*broken English*). Many Indians speak pigeon English.

Pile

Pile on — (*exaggerate*). Please do not pile on the statement.

To make one's pile — (*to earn as much as one needs*). The circumstances are such now-a-days that every one must try to make his pile.

Pill

A bitter pill to swallow — (*an insult*). His words are just a bitter pill to swallow which I cannot tolerate.

Pillar

From pillar to post — (*being driven from one difficulty to another*). The new job for Jatinder is from pillar to post.

Pillar of hope — (*faith*). Keep pillar of hope in God and you will succeed.

Pin

A pin — (*not at all*). I care a pin for money.

Pin-point — (*minute*). Threading the needle is a pinpoint job.

On one's pins — (*on one's legs*). After three years of struggle my son is now able to stand on his pins.

Pinch

Pinch of salt — (*with some caution*). Drive your car with a pinch of salt.

To know where the shoe pinches — (*to know the cause of trouble*). Only the wearer knows where the shoe pinches.

Pine

Done to pine — (*starved to death*). Many people were done to pine many in our country in 1942 famine.

Pine for — (*to desire for with grief*). The husband pined during his wife's absence.

Pipe

Piping hot — (*quite hot*). Let us have something piping hot.

To pipe one's eye — (*weep*). The child is piping his eye.

The time of piping peace — (*great peace*). The time of piping peace has almost vanished from the world's history now.

Pitfall

Pitfall — (*unexpected danger*). The Chinese invasion was a pitfall for India.

Place

To know one's place — (*to know one's position*). Before coming here, you should have known your place.

To make place — (*to give room*). Will you please make place for the old lady ?

Play

To play tricks — (*to try to deceive*). Never play tricks with your friends.

To play one's card well — (*make a good use of opportunities*). A wise is one who plays his cards well.

To play the fool — (*to act like a fool*). He played the fool in today's meeting.

To play the man — (*to act bravely*). Many soldiers play the man during the war.

Plough

To put one's hand to the plough — (*to undertake a task*). We are putting our hands to the plough on this new scheme.

Pluck

Pluck out — (*to draw out suddenly*). He had hardly spoken a word when his brother plucked out his tongue.

Pluck down — (*to demolish suddenly*). The whole city was plucked down by an earthquake just in three minutes.

Plunge

To take the plunge — (*to take the risk*). Come what may, you must take the plunge and appear in your exam.

Pocket

Out of pocket — (*to become poor*). Every salaried man is out of pocket on the last day of the month.

To have someone in one's pocket — (*completely under control*). The parents must have their children in pocket these days.

Point

To the point — (*relevant*). I am prepared to listen to any of your arguments provided they are to the point.

To point out — (*to find out*). The stitching of the shirt is so nice that you cannot point out any defect in it.

Poison

To poison one's ear's against — (*to set one against*). Never poison anyone's ears against your friends.

Post

To run your head against a post — (*to go to work as if you had no eyes*). While in office, be alert and do not run your head against a post.

Pot

Gone to pot — (*ruined*). Many families went to pot during the partition of the country.

Make the pot boil — (*to earn a living*). It is very hard to make the pot boil now-a-days.

A pot of money — (*a large amount of money*). A pot of money is required for doing this job.

Pot-belly — (*fat man*). Get away from my sight, I don't want to see a pot-belly.

Price

To set a price on one's head — (*to offer reward for capture*). A few years back the police had set a very heavy price on Man Singh's head.

Every man has his price — (*every man can be won by inducements*).

Prick

To prick one's ears — (*to pay particular attention*). Unless all of you prick your ears, you will not have any advantage of the principal's speech.

Proud

Proud as a peacock — (*very much proud*). The head of the department of this institution is as proud as a peacock.

Pull

To pull on — (*to live*). It is difficult to pull on with this meagre amount now-a-days.

To pull through — (*to get out of difficulty*). A little more effort and you will pull through this mess.

To pull to pieces — (*to criticise*). I do not like your habit of pulling to pieces everyone.

To pull about — (*to treat roughly*). Will you please stop pulling about that child's leg ?

Pulse

To feel one's pulse — (*to understand one's feeling*). Let us feel our pulse about him.

Purse

To put up a purse — (*to give a purse as prize*). Albert has put up a purse in his school on his getting first position in the class.

Purse-proud — (*puffed up with money*). Do not be a purse-proud fellow.

Push

To give one the push — (*to dismiss from service*). The manager of your company has given the push to the new clerk.

To push through — (*to bring to confusion*). Please do not push through your statement.

To make a push — (*to try*). There is no harm in the making a push in the examination.

to push up — (*give promotion*). Jatindra has not been pushed up in his seven years of service.

Put

Put-off — (*postpone*). Let us put off the meeting till tomorrow.

To put up with — (*to bear*). I cannot put up with your silly arguments.

Put on — (*wear*). You look very beautiful when you are putting on this green saree.

Put two and two together — (*to draw a conclusion from the simple facts*). Since everything is now clear before us, it is easy to put two and two together and get the result.

Quality

People of quality — (*upper classes*). You must learn to move with people of quality.

The quality of a defect — (*good mixed with evil*). His rude speech with a good heart is the quality of a defect.

Quantity

Pure quantity — (*numbers*). The pure quantity of men was very poor in the whole gathering.

Quarrel

To pick up a quarrel — (*to seek occasion for fighting*). Pakistanis are always on the lookout for picking up a quarrel with Indians.

To take up a quarrel — (*to settle a dispute*). Even the U.N. is unable to take up a quarrel of India and Pakistan over the 'Kashmir issue'.

Find quarrel in a straw — (*be captious*). Your habit of finding quarrel in a straw is no good.

To quarrel with your bread and butter — (*to act in a way which harms your interests*). It is foolish to quarrel with one's bread and butter.

Quarter

From all quarters — (*from all sides*). He is deprived of a service from all quarters.

To take one's quarter — (*to lodge*). We are going to take up our quarter in Mumbai.

Queen

Queen mother — (*mother of ruler*). The queen mother should always guide the king on proper lines.

Queen Anne is dead — (*a remark made for a person who gives stale news*).

Queen of Grace — (*virgin Mary*). Worship the Queen of Grace and she will bless you to succeed in your mission.

Queer

In queer street — (*in debt*). Throughout his life, his father lived in queer street.

Query

To suppress query — (*to hide facts*). Please make us know of the true statement and do not suppress query.

Quest

In quest of — (*in search of*). In quest of his son, he met with a car accident and died in on the spot.

To quest about — (*to go in search*). What have you gone to quest about ?

Question

Out of question — (*not worth discussing*). It is out of question for me to accept my wife now.

To call in question — (*to challenge*). Can you accept the call in question given by him ?

To put a question to — (*to ask something*). Every student is at liberty to put a question to his teacher.

Oblique question — (*indirect question*). India always gets an oblique question from Pakistan.

Quick

To the quick — (*to the heart*). I am touched to the quick by your misbehaviour.

The quick and the dead — (*the living and the dead*). The quick and the dead have no uniformity.

To cut to the quick — (*to hurt bitterly*). Your taunts are cutting to the quick, please stop speaking.

Quick-witted — (*intelligent*). The quick-witted man of the class has died.

Quiet

On the quiet — (*in meditation*). She is on the quiet now-a-days.

To have a quiet dig — (*to taunt gently*). The wise is one who has a quiet dig in society.

Quip

To make quips — (*utter sarcastic remarks*). Will you please stop making quips now ?

Quit

To quit oneself well — (*to behave well*). He did not quit himself well in yesterday's party.

Quits

To be on quits with — (*on equal terms*). They are both on quits with one another.

Rabid

Rabid hate — (*great hate*). He has now developed a rabid hate for his wife.

Rabid democrat — (*unreasoning democrat*). No one likes the rabid democrats.

Rack

To rack one's brains — (*to strain one's thoughts to the utmost*). I have already racked my brains, you don't expect me to tax more.

To go to the rack and ruin — (*complete destruction*). In war many nations go to rack and ruin.

On the rack — (*in distress*). His failing business has resulted in going the whole of his family on the rack.

Racket

To stand the racket — (*to come successfully through test*). He is capable of standing any racket.

Radical

Radical error — (*fundamental mistake*). Such radical errors will ruin your career one day.

Radical change, reform or cure — (*fundamental : right from the root*). Unless a radical change takes place in the country, the Government will not improve.

Radical idea — (*basic principles*). Mahatma Gandhi preached the radical idea of non-violence.

Rags

In rags — (*in torn clothes*). When he returned home, he was all in rags.

Rail

Off the rail — (*disorganised*). Do not disturb me, my mind is off the rail now-a-days.

Rain

A rainy day — (*bad days*). We should always have something for the rainy days.

To rain cats and dogs — (*to rain very heavily*). It is raining cats and dogs for the last four days.

Rains or shine — (*in small weathers*). he is very strict on his promise; don't worry, he will come here rains or shine.

It never rains but pours — (*events usually happen together*).

Raise

To raise the banner — (*to lead*). Who will raise the banner ?

To raise from the dead — (*to restore to life*). The doctor was able to raise the baby from the dead.

To raise the wind — (*to procure money for some purpose*). The Government is raising the wind for the Indira Gandhi Memorial Trust.

To raise hell — (*to create confusion*). You are always raising a hell for us.

Ram

To ram into — (*to force*). You cannot ram education into your children.

Rank

Rank with — (*be of the same standard*). Pandit Nehru ranked with the top dignitaries of the world.

Rank and file — (*common soldiers*). Many rank and file lose their lives in war.

Rap

Not worth a rap — (*not worth even a half penny, useless*). The old man is not worth a rap.

Rap on the knuckles — (*a nice beating*). The thief was given a rap on the knuckles by the police but to no avail.

Rapture

To go into raptures — (*to drive to extreme delight*). After seeing the film all the spectators went into raptures.

Rat

To smell a rat — (*to suspect*). The police is smelling a rat at our neighbour's house about last night's theft.

Rate

At any rate — (*any how*). I must get this job done at any rate.

At the rate of — (*at the speed of*). The car is running at the rate of 30 km. per hour.

Rather

Rather better than — (*somewhat in excess*). He is earning rather better than his brother.

Raw

Raw youth — (*inexperienced*). Do not appoint a raw youth in your company; he will not be of much use to you.

Touch one in raw — (*wound one's feeling*). Today's speech of the principal has touched every student in the raw.

Raw spirits — (*strong drinks*). Do not indulge in raw spirits.

Ray

Ray of hope — (*some hope*). If you have even a ray of hope, you should sit for the examination.

Razor

Razor edge — (*a dangerous position*). Our country is passing through a razor-edge these days.

Read

Read one's meaning — (*comprehend*). Please read the meaning of this book.

Read a riddle — (*to solve it*). Can you read this riddle.

Really

Really and truly — (*positively*) really and truly, we shall be able to complete the job by evening.

Reap

To reap the fruit of — (*to enjoy the consequences of*). You will have to reap the fruits of your doings.

To sow wind and reap whirlwind — (*the result of bad actions is necessarily bad*). When you are sowing wind you will naturally reap whirlwind only.

To reap where one has not sown — (*to profit by other's toil*). In politics, many become lucky of reaping where they have not sown.

Rear

To bring up the rear — (*to come last*). In this planning of family budget, the clothes brought up the rear.

To hang on the rear of — (*to follow with a view to attack*). The Chinese have been hanging on the rear of India.

Reason

By reason of — (*on account of*). By reason of one's hard labour, one is bound to succeed in life.

Recede

Recede from — (*withdraw*). The stand taken by us is such that if we recede from it, we shall be much insulted.

Reckon

To reckon on — (*to depend*). You can easily reckon on his work.

Reckon with — (*to call to account*). It is high time that you should reckon with your manager or else he will deceive you one day.

The day of reckoning — (*the day of judgement*). The criminal absented himself from the court on the day of reckoning.

Record

Matter of record — (*established as a fact*). You cannot deny this matter of record.

Beat or break the record — (*to outdo the highest achievement*). Your friend has broken the record in the long race.

Off the record — (*unofficially, not intended for publication*). The new clerk's appointment is off the record.

Recover

To recover one's senses — (*to regain consciousness*). He has recovered his senses after three days.

Red

Red-handed — (*one the spot*). The manager was caught red-handed while being bribed.

Don't care a red cent — (*don't care at all*). I don't care a red cent for you.

Red-tape — (*official formality*). It is high time that red-tapism should disappear at higher levels.

Reduce

Reduce to ashes — (*to go to waste*). The fire has reduced the whole city to ashes.

Reduce to the rank — (*to degrade for misconduct*). The senior clerk of the office has been reduce to the rank this afternoon.

Reed

A broken reed — (*an unreliable person*). You cannot depend upon him, he is simply a broken reed.

Reference

With reference to — (*in connection with*). With reference to your postcard of today, we have despatched the goods by rail.

Reflect

To reflect upon — (*to affect*). Your laziness reflects upon your health.

Refuge

To take refuge — (*to find shelter*). Till you get a suitable accommodation you can take refuge at our place.

Rein

To rein one's anger — (*to control one's anger*). Please rein your anger if you want to work here.

Relation

To relation to — (*as compared with*). In relation to Mohan, Sohan is quite weak in his studies.

Relegate

To relegate to the past — (*forget*). We can never relegate to the past the partition of our country.

Relieve

To relieve one of — (*to deprive one of*). The thief relieved him of his watch.

Rely

To rely upon — (*to depend*). India can never rely upon the faithfulness of Pakistan.

Render

Render to — (*give in return*). Can you render your services to me for two rupees ?

Render into — (*translate*). The foreign ambassador's whole speech was rendered into Hindustani afterwards.

Repeat

History repeats itself — (*old events recur again and again*).

Respect

To pay one's respects — (*to compliment*). Please pay my respects to your elders.

Responsibility

To shoulder the responsibility — (*to be responsible for*). I am prepared to shoulder the responsibility of educating you.

Sense of responsibility — (*to feel that one has to perform any duty assigned to him*). Sense of responsibility is realized by a very few in our country.

Rest

For the rest — (*as regards other matter*). For the rest, do not worry, I shall do everything myself.

Retard

To retard the progress of — (*to check*). The death of his father was responsible for retarding his progress in studies.

Retract

To retract from one's promise — (*to go back on one's word*). Come what may, one must not retract from one's promise.

Rhyme

Without rhyme or reason — (*without proper cause*). Never say anything to your child without rhyme or reason.

Rid

To get rid of — (*to save oneself from*). I just want to get rid of him.

Riddle

To be riddled with — (*full of*). The whole body was riddled with bullets.

Ride

To ride for a fall — (*to proceed with one's business without caring for its consequences*). It is unwise to ride for a fall; one must always be cautious.

To ride a whirlwind — (*to direct a mighty force*). The Chief Minister is riding a whirlwind for establishing a new factory for his sons.

To ride on the shoulder of — (*to use the power and influence of*). If you ride on the shoulder of your brother, you can get this job at any moment.

Right

Right and left — (*both sides*). While on road always look to right and left.

Right-hand man — (*a confidential assistant*). The manager has dismissed his right-hand man.

Send right about — (*send sacking*). Please send right about that clerk; he is good for nothing.

Right and might — (*justice and power*). Right and might side with truth

Ring

Ringleader — (*the chief used in bad sense*). Who is the ringleader of all this nonsense?

To make rings round one — (*to defeat a person completely in a competition, etc.*). Late Krishana Menon made rings round Kripalani during the last election.

Riot

To run riot — (*to lose and control*). The principal has run riot on his teachers in the school.

Rise

The rising generation — (*the young people*). The rising generation of our country must be prepared to work hard.

One's soul to rise against — (*to find it intolerable*). Your statement is merely your soul's rise against mine.

To get a rise — (*to get a promotion*). He is likely to get a rise in office.

Road

The rules of the road — (*etiquetter*). If you want to rise in life you must learn the rules of the road.

On the road — (*progressing towards*). He is on the road in his new business.

Rock

On the rocks — (*no money*). A clerk is generally on the rocks during the last days of the month.

Rod

To kiss the rod — (*to submit to the punishment without any murmur*). The thief is prepared to kiss the rod.

Make something a rod for one's back — (*to prepare trouble for oneself*). By going there, you made something a rod for your back.

Roll

Roll of honour — (*list of those who have died for the country*). The complete Roll of Honour during the Chinese aggression is yet to be published by the Government.

A rolling stone gathers no mass — (*a person who changes his profession too often is generally unsuccessful*).

To strike off the rolls — (*to debar from practising on account of dishonesty*). The Chartered Accountants Association has struck off the rolls Messers A.B & Co.

Rome

Do in Rome as the Romans do — (*adopt yourself to your surroundings*).

Rome was not built in a day — (*encouragement to the faint-hearted*).

Roost

To rule the roost — (*be master*). The old man rules the roost in our home.

Go to the roost — (*retire for the night*). I am in the habit of going to roost early.

Root

The root of the matter — (*its base*). Unless we are convinced of the facts of the root of the matter, we cannot proceed further.

To strike roots — (*to get established*). Now we have struck roots of our business fully.

Root and branch — (*the whole of it without any omission or exception*). Will you please do the job root and branch.

Rope

To know the ropes — (*to become familiar to all tricks*). It is very difficult to know the ropes of the British policy.

Rope of sand — (*delusive security*). Money is at best a rope of sand.

To rope in (*to make one to take part in some enterprise*). It is high time that you should now rope in Ramesh.

Rose

A bed of roses — (*a pleasant experience*). Life is not a bed of roses.

Under the rose — (*under strict confidence*). The whole discussion is under the rose.

To be not all roses — (*not to be pure enjoyment*). Everything in the world is not all roses.

To gather roses — (*to seek pleasure*). Please stop the habit of gathering roses and do something solid.

Path strewn with roses — (*life of delight*). Path strewn with roses is available for the very rich only.

Rot

Left to rot — (*left to suffer*). By his going to Mumbai his whole family has been left to rot.

Rotten

Rotten egg — (*a useless person*). The manager has been instructed to check out all the rotton eggs from the office.

Round

A good round sum — (*a large sum of money*). The Government is spending a good round sum on planning only.

Round dealing — (*honest and straightforward*). A business man with round dealings is always successful in life.

Rough

To be rough with — (*to treat harshly*). The police are always rough with thieves.

Rough and tumble — (*irregular*). The company has issued termination notices to all rough and tumble employees.

To have a rough time — (*to suffer cruelty*). Many nations have had to go through a rough time during the war.

Rub

Without rub or interruption — (*without any obstruction*). I was able to get this good post without rub or interruption.

To rub the wrong way — (*to irritate*). Your habit of rubbing the wrong way is not liked by any member of our club.

To rub one's hands — (*to show satisfaction*). When he learnt that his son got second division in the Matriculation examination, he rubbed his hands.

Ruin

To bring to ruin — (*to cause destruction*). The Nagas are bent upon bringing to ruin the Indian borders.

Run

In the long run — (*ultimately*). Honesty wins in the long run.

To run the show — (*to successfully manage some establishment*). Our proprietor runs the show of office himself.

On the run — (*moving from place to place as a fugitive*). Since losing his job he has been on the run for the last six months.

Rush

Not worth a rush — (*useless*). I don't know how he has been appointed as Secretary : He is not worth a rush.

S

Sack

To be sacked — (*dismissed*). The new clerk has been sacked because of dishonesty.

In sack-cloth and ashes — (*in mourning or penitential garb*). Do not go for interview in sack-cloth and ashes.

Sad

In sad earnest — (*seriously*). Please do not laugh. I am telling you everything in sad earnest.

Saddle

In the saddle — (*in office*). One must perform one's duties properly in the saddle.

To put the saddle on the right horse — (*to blame the right person*). By dismissing his P.A., the manager has put the saddle on the right horse.

Safe

Safe and sound — (*secure*). The life of Indians is not safe and sound in Pakistan.

Sail

Take in sail — (*moderate one's ambition*). It is high time that you should take in sail if you want to rise in life.

To sail close to the wind — (*to break a moral principle*). If our leaders sail close to the wind what will the public do?

To sail under false colours — (*to pretend what one is not*). The teacher sailed under false colours and was dismissed from service.

Sake

For one's namesake — (*out of consideration for one's good name*). You should not indulge in such habits for your namesake at least.

To eat one's salt — (*to be one's guest*). He is eating our salt now-a-days..

True to his salt — (*faithfull to his boss*). It is difficult to get a servant who is true to his salt.

To take with a pinch of salt — (*to be incredulous*). The company is taking up the union's matter with a pinch of salt.

Sam

To stand Sam — (*to pay*). Every parent has to stand Sam for his children.

Sand

A rope of sand — (*something nominally effective and strong*). The government laws regarding corruption seem to be a rope of sand in our country.

Sands are running out (*time is nearly at an end*). Sands are running out for the Matric examination.

Sandwich

A sandwich of good and bad — (*mixture of good and evil*). The notorious dacoit, Man Singh was a sandwich of good and bad.

Satire

To be satire upon — (*to contradict*). People like you are merely a satire upon our society.

Sauce

Without the sauce of — (*without the interest of*). Without the sauce of promotions and ambitions one can never be successful in life.

Save

To save the situation — (*to provide a way out of difficulty*). He saved the situation by reaching there in time.

Say

To say a good word for — (*recommend*). If you just say a good word for me, I am sure to get this job.

To say one nay — (*refuse anything*). The parents are so disgusted that they will say nay to Danesh now.

Scale

To turn the scales — (*to outweigh the other side*). Pandit Nehru's speech always turned the scales of other parties.

Hold the scales even — (*impartial*). Our Government is holding the scales even for all the communities in the country.

Scandal

A scandalous state of affairs — (*most shocking circumstances*). A scandalous state of affairs exists in many ministeries.

Scarce

To make himself scarce — (*to retire*). He has made himself scarce from the service now.

Scheme

Scheme of colours — (*plan for doing something*). They have a scheme of colours for establishing a new factory at Chandigarh.

School

School of adversity — (*poor circumstances*). The whole family is passing through the school of adversity now-a-days.

Scissors

Scissors and paste — (*compilation work*). Mr. C. Anand is an expert scissors-and-paste.

Scores

To pay off old scores — (*to revenge an injury*). Behave well with every one and do not give anyone an opportunity to pay off old scores.

Scrap

On the scrap-heap — (*thrown aside as worm out*). Prohibition rules in many cities are now on the scrap-heap.

Scratch

Scratch of the pen — (*signature of written order*). Rich people do a lot just by the scratch of their pen.

To scratch one's face — (*to attack directly*). The Chinese have no guts to scratch their face.

Screw

There is a screw loose somewhere — (*all is not right*). There is a screw loss in every society.

To screw up one's courage — (*to gather resolution*). The coming generation has to screw up its courage to face the coming hard days.

To press on the screw — (*to press for payment*). Let us first press on the screw and then see what he has to say.

His head is screwed on the right way — (*he is quite an intelligent person and knows what he is after*).

Scrub

To want a good scrub — (*thorough cleaning*). Every Government wants a good scrub at regular intervals.

Sea

To be at sea — (*confused*). You must be firm-minded; it is no use being at sea always.

Seal

Seal of love — (*kiss*). Since his marriage, for the last three months, he has never put a seal of love to his wife.

Set one's seal to — (*to give one's authority or assent to*). The President has set his seal to the Emergency Ordinance.

Give under my hand and seal — (*under my signature*). This new plan has been given under my hand and seal.

Secular

Secular fame — (*enduring reputation*). Very few leaders enjoy a secular fame.

See

To see through — (*to help*). Can you see me through my difficulty ?

Please see to it — (*please look well to it*).

To see the light — (*to be published*). Our book on idioms will see the light next month.

To see off — (*to go to bid farewell*). We want to see off our Manager at the railway station.

I will see about it — (*I will consider it*).

Seek

To seek after or for — (*to follow*). We should seek after ideal principles of the Congress.

To seek one's fortune — (*to advance position in life, to try luck*). He is bent upon seeking his fortune these days.

Self

To be beside one's self — (*to be out of control*). The teachers should always see that the students are never beside themselves.

Send

To send one to the right about — (*to dismiss unceremoniously*). The peon has been sent to the right about for his misbehaviour.

To send word — (*to send a message*). The manager sent a word through peon to his wife.

A warm send-off — (*grand farewell*). On Sinha's transfer to Delhi, the whole staff of our office gave him a warm send-off.

Sense

Out of senses — (*mad*). Do not talk to that man; he is always out of senses.

Sensual pleasure — (*joy of the flesh*). Those who live for the sensual pleasure are never successful in life.

Serve

To serve one out — (*to distribute*). Serve out the sweet among the children.

To serve one's turn — (*to suit one's purpose*). The new employee serves his turn in the office.

Set

Set in — (*begin*). Will you please set in with the job?

To set onself against — (*oppose*). I have no guts to set myself against his arguments.

Set apart — (*to reserve*). We must set apart some thing for a rainy day.

Set purpose — (*great determination*). Shastriji was a man of set purpose.

Set by — (*save*). Set by something for a rainy day.

Seven

At sixes and sevens — (*at loggerheads*). All the members of this club are always at sixes and sevens.

Shadow

Shadow factory — (*a factory built for emergency*). Many shadow factories were introduced during the recent National Emergency.

Share

To share one's last crust — (*to give away everything*). Acharya Vinoba Bhave has shared his last crust.

Sharp

Sharp practice — (*dishonesty*). Sharp practice never pays.

Look sharp — (*act quickly*). Raju always looks sharp.

Sheep

Sheep and goats — (*good and bad*). Sheep and goats always go together.

Sheep's eye — (*a living, wishful glance*). He gave a sheep's eye to his wife.

Sheep that have no shepherd — (*helpless crowd*). Pakistani people are sheep that have no shepherd.

Shell

Shell out — (*to hand over*). Please shell out his file to me.

To come out of one's shell — (*to throw off reserve*). The rat was at last able to come out of his shell.

Shift

The shift and changes of life — (*ups and downs*).

To shift off — (*to put away*). The meeting has been shifted off from tomorrow.

Shine

Put a good shine on — (*to make a good show*). Let us put a good shine on the stage.

To take the shine out of — (*to impair brilliance*). His employer has taken his shine out.

Shirt

To keep one's shirt — (*to maintain temper*). Please keep your shirt and listen to us.

To give one a wet shirt — (*to work on till he sweats*). The labourers in our country are being given a wet shirt by their employers.

Shoe

To know where the shoe pinches — (*to know the cause of the trouble*). Only wearer knows where the shoe pinches.

Dead man's shoes — (*dead man's property*). The dead man's shoes are being auctioned in the market.

To step into someone's shoes — (*to assume responsibilities*). The new Government is stepping into the shoes of the old one.

To put the shoe on the right foot — (*to lay the blame where it rightly belongs*). By taking Jatinder to task the principal has put the shoe on the right foot.

Shoot

A shooting pain — (*a quick, sharp pain*). I have a shooting pain in my back.

Shop

To talk shop — (*to talk business*). If you are free we can talk shop now.

To come to the wrong shop — (*to apply to the wrong person*). By calling Brij Mohan to this place, you have come to the wrong shop.

Shoulder

To shoulder a responsibility — (*to face a great task*). The parents have to shoulder so many responsibilities for their children.

Shoulder to shoulder — (*with heart and action*). In order to complete this job in time we must work shoulder to shoulder.

To put one's shoulder to the wheel — (*to help*). Our neighbours are putting shoulders to the wheels of all the persons of our street.

Short

The long and short — (*conclusion*). The long and short of the matter is that we will not go there.

Show

To show up — (*to expose*). Please do not show up this in the sun or else it will get spoiled.

To show off — (*to display*). Our books have been shown off in the racks of good booksellers.

Shut

Shut out — (*to prevent from entering*). The principal ordered the peon to shut out Ramesh from the room.

Shut in — (*to enclose*). A few rupees are shut in the envelope for purchasing the return ticket.

Side

Side by side — (*at the same time*). Let us try to complete this ledger also side by side.

Sight

To lose sight of — (*to overlook*). Do not lose sight of minor events, sometimes they are very important in one's life.

Out of sight, out of mind — (*said, when something is forgotten for not having been seen for a pretty long time*).

Silence

To put silence — (*to refuse an argument*). The students put the professor to silence.

To pass into silence — (*to die*). The old man has passed into silence.

Six

To be at sixes and sevens — (*to be in disorder*). When we returned home we found everything at sixes and sevens.

Skim

To skim the cream off — (*to take the best part*). She skimmed the cream off the whole show.

Skin

Save one's skin — (*to escape without injury*). During the partition all the persons of our street were able to save their skins.

Change one's skin — (*to undergo impossible changes*). He talks all nonsense; he cannot change his skin.

To the skin — (*completely*). When the doctor arrived he was wet in blood to the skin.

Escape with the skin of one's teeth — (*narrowly*). Many of us escaped with the skin of our teeth during the partition of the country.

Sleep

Let sleeping dogs lie — (*avoid stirring up trouble*).

Sleeve

To roll up one's sleeves — (*to get ready to fight*). The Chinese rolled up their sleeves in 1962 against India.

To laugh one's sleeves — (*to laugh privately*). It is wise to laugh in one's sleeves.

Slip

Slip of tongue — (*a slight mistake in speaking*). Be very careful in your speech, a slip of the tongue can cause enormous harm.

Solid

To be solid with — (*to have a firm footing with*). He is solid with his service.

Some

Somehow or other — (*anyhow*). I will get this job somehow or the other.

Sorry

To cut a sorry figure — (*to be subjected to shame*). When he found the principal coming to his room be had to cut a sorry figure.

A sorry fellow — (*mean fellow*). I have stopped talking to such sorry fellows.

Soup

In the soup — (*in difficulty*). The whole family is in soup now-a-days.

Spin

To spin a yarn — (*to tell a story*). Please stop spinning yarn and tell us something which is true.

Stand

To stand against — (*to withstand*). I cannot stand against him.

Stand by — (*to support*). Please stand by me in my trouble.

Stone

At a stone's throw — (*quite near*). When we were discussing about his marriage, he was standing at a stone's throw.

To leave no stone unturned — (*to do everything to achieve something*). If I am given this job I shall leave no stone unturned to give you every satisfaction.

Store

In store — (*hoard for future use*). Let us keep something in store.

Table

Under the table — (*in a position lower than*). When we returned home, we found him under the table.

Tailor

Tailor makes the man — (*man is judged by his clothes*).

Take

To take hand in — (*to interfere*). Do not take hand in other's affairs.

To take to heels — (*to run away*). On seeing the policeman, the thief took to his heels.

To take off — (*to put off*). Please take off your wet coat.

To take on — (*to be extremely affected or upset*). The Prime Minister's statement took on the whole Parliament.

Tall

Tall talk — (*only words and no actions*). He is simply a man of tall talk, he cannot be anything in reality.

Tar

Tarred with the same brush — (*having the same faults*). The whole club of our locality is tarred with the same brush.

Tea

A tea fight — (*a tea party*). On his success in the examination he is arranging a tea fight, this evening.

Tear

To tear up by the roots — (*to destroy completely*). The earthquake has torn up the whole city by the roots.

Teeny

Teeny-weeny — (*Very small*). His teeny-weeny son has been overrun by a car.

Teeth

In the teeth of opposition — (*in the face of*). In the teeth of opposition from his classmates, he lost the chance of senatorship.

Tell

To tell upon — (*to affect*). His hard labour has told upon his health.

Ten

Ten to one — (*chances are quite high*). Ten to one are the chances of your success; you must appear in your exam.

Tenor

The tenor of one's life — (*direction*). You have absolutely no right to interfere in the tenor of her life.

Term

To come to terms — (*to make an agreement*). Unless China and India come to terms, there is every possibility of war beginning again.

Test

To take a test — (*to appear in the examination*). I shall be taking my final test by the end of this month.

To give a test — (*to examine*). The college is giving a test to all the new entrants.

That

This and that — (*odds and ends*). Do not waste your time in this and that.

Then

Then and there — (*at the very place and time*). The thieves caught hold of my friend and robbed him then and there.

Thick

Through thick and thin — (*under all conditions*). Promise to stand by you through thick and thin.

Thick-headed — (*stupid*). It is no use talking to that thick-headed fellow.

Lay it on thick — (*be profuse in compliments*). The flatterers get their ends by laying it on thick.

Think

To give something to think — (*to think about*). Develop the habit of giving something to think among your children.

Thorn

To sit on the thorns — (*to be continuously in trouble*). Ever since I left that job I am sitting on the thorns for the last two years.

To have a thorn in one's flesh — (*a constant source of irritation*). Your presence is simply a thorn in my flesh.

Thorough

Thorough paced — (*complete*). He is a good worker and you can always expect a thorough paced work from him.

Thousand

Thousand and one — (*numberless*). Thousand and one are the animals in our country but only a few are good.

One in a thousand — (*rare*). The diamond offered for sale at this counter is one in a thousand.

Thrash

To thrash a point home — (*to make one understand*). Our new principal is not intelligent enough to thrash a point home.

To thrash a matter out — (*to discuss a subject from all angles*). Let us all sit together and thrash the matter out.

Thread

Threadbare — (*completely*). When he returned home we discussed the problem threadbare.

Lost the thread — (*lost the link*). In listening to him I just lost the thread of your speech, please repeat what you said.

To hang by a thread — (*to be in a precarious state*). The patient's life is hanging by a thread.

Throat

To cut one's throat — (*to kill*). During the partition, throats of many Hindus and Muslims were cut.

Through

Through and through — (*completely*). His father is through and through in debt now-a-days.

Throw

To throw out — (*to remove by force*). The manager ordered the peon to throw out the new clerk on account of his misbehaviour.

At a stone's throw — (*quite near*). When we were discussing about his marriage, he was standing only at a stone's throw.

Those who live in glass houses should not throw stones at others — (*do not find fault with others when you have faults yourself*).

Thrum

Thread and thrum — (*all alike; good and bad*). Our Government has a thread and thrum behaviour with all classes of people.

Thumb

Under the thumb of — (*under one's influence*). This job is under the thumb of your brother; if he wants he can oblige me.

Rule of thumb — (*something done through merely a rough guess work*). No Government can last long under the rule of thumb.

Tick

On the tick — (*with exact punctuality*). He is always on the tick in office.

Tide

To tide over difficulty (*to surmount it by sheer circumstances and not any personal hard endeavours*).

To take at a tide — (*to take at the best possible moment*). Be wise and take everything at the tide.

Time and tide — (*opportunities*). Once in life the times and tide knocks the door of everyone.

To go with the tide — (*to follow the masses*). One should always think and not simply go with the tide.

Tidy

Neat and tidy — (*absolutely clean*). In honour of the foreign Prime Minister the whole city has been made neat and tidy.

Tie

Tie of blood — (*blood relationship*). Just a little misunderstanding lost the tie of blood among them.

Tight

To be in a tight corner — (*to be in a difficult situation*). Since I lost that job, our whole family is in a tight corner.

Tight-fitted — (*stingy*). A tight-fitted fellow is not liked by anyone.

Tip

Tip-top — (*first rate*). Our office always maintains tip-top cleanliness.

To have at one's fingertips — (*to remember thoroughly*). He has mathematics at his fingertips.

Tip and run raid — (*sudden attack and instantaneous disappearance with the booty*). Tip and run raids are increasing all the world over day by day.

Tittle

Tittle-tattle — (*gossip*). Everybody is not fond of tittle-tattle.

To

To and fro — (*here and there*). On reaching home we found the things scattered to and fro.

Toe

To toe the line — (*to confirm under pressure*). The whole staff toed the line of the manager.

To tread on one's toe — (*to offend one's feelings*). By entering into a pact with China, Pakistan had tread on the toes of India.

From top to toe — (*from head to foot*). He is gentle from top to toe.

Toll

To take in the toll — (*to ensure*). The Government is planning to take all the candidates in the toll.

Tomorrow

Today and tomorrow — (*present and future*). Earn sufficient to spend today and tomorrow.

Tongue

To be on the tongues of men — (*much talked of*). Pandit Nehru is on the tongues of men.

To hold one's tongues — (*to keep silent*). Unless somebody asks you to give your suggestions, you must hold your tongue.

Too

It is too good to be true — (*unbelievable*) this is such a good news that I can't believe it is true).

It is never too late to mend — (*improvement is always possible*).

Tooth

In the teeth of (*against*). Do not go in the teeth of your parent's opposition.

Armed to the teeth — (*armed completely*). The soldiers at the border are always armed to the teeth.

To fight tooth and nail — (*with great violence*). Every army has to fight tooth and nail in war.

To show one's teeth — (*to adopt a threatening attitude*). Since that happening our manager always shows his teeth in the office.

Torch

To hand on the torch — (*to keep knowledge alive*). Let us join hands together and make efforts to hand on the torch.

Tread

Tread in the footsteps of — (*to follow the examples of*). Let us tread in the footsteps of Pandit Nehru.

Turn

To turn up — (*to happen*). It is no use waiting for him, he will never turn up.

To have turn for — (*fitness*). My brother has turn for cricket only.

To turn one's coat — (*to change to the opposite side*). Many political leaders are clever enough to turn their coats at times.

Ugly

An ugly situation — (*in an awkward position*). Your today's speech in the college has put the whole class in an ugly situation.

Ugly duckling — (*a person who turns out to be a genius of the family after being thought a dullard*).

Under

Under the mark — (*inferior*). People under the mark find hard to live in modern society.

Under a cloud — (*in suspicion*). He has been arrested just under a cloud.

Under the sun — (*anywhere*). Even a beggar has some place under the sun to live.

Under lock and key — (*in safe custody*). We have kept all our cash and ornaments under lock and key.

Understanding

To come to an understanding — (*to agree*). Let us come to an understanding and end the matter once and for all.

Unity

Unity of idea — (*coherence of thought*). Unity of my ideas is affected by your silly arguments.

To be at unity with — (*to be in harmony with*). The husband and wife are at unity with each other.

Until

Until and unless — (*under condition*). Until and unless you come, we will not go.

Up

Up and down — (*here and there*). The servants have searched the child up and down in the house but he is nowhere.

Up-to-date — (*complete*). His accounts are never up-to-date.

Ups and downs — (*misfortunes*). Ups and downs are always there in one's life.

On the up and up — (*improving*). Since taking that medicine the patient is on the up and up every moment.

Upside

Upside down — (*in total disorder*). The child has put all my files and other office papers upside down.

Use

Of no use — (*useless*). Your offer is of no use to me now, I have failed in my examination.

Use and wont — (*custom and habit*). One should always try to be happy according to use and wont.

Utility

Public utility — (*of great use to public*). Electricity is a great public utility.

Utmost

To do one's utmost — (*to do one's best*). Unless you do your utmost, you will not succeed in your exam.

Utter

Utter failure — (*extreme failure*). He is an utter failure in Hockey.

Utter disgust — (*extreme displeasure*). Your mark sheet is an utter disgust for the whole family.

Utterance

To give utterance to — (*express*). Please give utterance to your view.

V

Vacant

Vacant frivolities — (*useless enjoyment*). Stop in dulging in vacant frivolities, if you want to rise in life.

Vamp

To vamp up an old story — (*to refurbish an old story*). Some newspapers just vamp up old stories.

Van

In the van of — (*at the head of*). In the van of this institution is its president.

Variance

To be at variance with — (*different from*). Pakistan is generally a variance with Indian suggestions regarding settlement of the Kashmir problem.

Veil

Beyond the veil — (*in the unknown state after death*). Nobody knows what happens beyond the veil.

To raise the veil — (*uncover*). He has raised the veil and truth is now known to everyone.

To draw a veil over — (*to avoid discussing*). Let us draw a veil over the old matter and start afresh.

Velvet

On velvet — (*in an advantageous position*). In the tennis match, Surinder of our college is always on velvet.

Velvet glove — (*outward gentleness cloaking inflexibility*). Diplomacy is velvet glove.

Vent

To give vent to — (*to give full expression*). Please see that you give vent to your ideas in the meeting.

Verge

On the verge of — (*on the point of*). His brother is on the verge of death.

Vest

To vest with — (*furnish*). Many Asian countries interest is vested with each other.

Vestige

The vestige — (*evidence of*). The vestige of the fact exists in the criminal's statement.

Vice

Vice versa — (*the other way round*). You may go there vice versa, I shall come.

Vice of the constitution — (*physical defect*). Every human being has some vice of the constitution.

Vie

To vie with — (*compete*). Yusuf is poor enough to vie with other candidates.

View

In view of — (*having regard to*). In view of what he is doing, he needs a promotion in the office.

Beyond the view — (*which cannot be seen*). Just within five minutes the train went beyond the view from the railway station.

To come to view — (*to be seen*). The ship has now come to view.

Point of view — (*opinion*). His point of view differs much from ours.

Violent

To lay violent hands on — (*to beat*). The thief laid violent hands on Seth and ran away with five thousand rupees.

Virtue

By virtue of — (*by reason of*). By virtue of his past excellent record he has been promoted as the manager of our factory.

Vista

To open a new vista — (*to show new prospects*). The Government has opened many new vistas for young men of our country.

Visits

To play a visit — (*to go and meet*). During my sickness, he paid me a visit daily.

Voice

With one voice — (*Unanimously*). The new President was elected with one voice by the Congress Party.

To give voice to (*express*). All the members of the club have equal rights to give voice to their feelings.

Wade

Wade through book — (*read it despite dullness*). I cannot wade through this book.

Wade into — (*attack energitically*). The Chinese waded into Indian territory recently.

Wait

To wait upon — (*to attend to*). The waiters of small restaurants generally do not wait well upon their patrons.

To lie in wait — (*ambush*). Failure lies in wait for lazy lads.

Wake

In the wake of — (*behind*). In the wake of success are many failures too.

Walk

Walk into — (*thrash; abuse*). Please stop walking into his arguments.

To walk the streets — (*to be a prostitute*). Poverty has compelled many young women of our country to walk the streets.

Wall

To go to the wall — (*to be defeated*). One party has to go to the wall in war.

To run one's head against the wall — (*attempt impossibilities*). If you just leave the habit of running your head against the wall, I am sure you can rise to a good position in life.

War

To wage a war — (*to launch a war*). The Chinese waged a war against India in 1962.

Dogs of war — (*havoc attending war*). The dogs of war should never be let loose.

War to the knife — (*struggle to the bitter end*). Dara Singh is strong enough to war to his knife.

Warm

A warm corner — (*a hot part of battle*). The days have gone when Japan as a warm corner of Asia.

To make things warm for one — (*to create strong feelings against one*). Never make things warm for your friends.

To give warm reception — (*to welcome enthusiastically*). Wherever Pandit Nehru went, he was given a warm reception.

Wash

To wash one's dirty linen in public — (*to accuse each other in public*). The wise are those who avoid washing their dirty linen in public.

To wash one's hands of — (*to give up altogether*). I have washed the hands of my hope for getting through in the examination.

Watch

To pass as a watch in the night — (*to be forgotten soon*). Rest assured, our friendship will never be passed as a watch in the night.

On the watch — (*waiting*). Please hurry up, the taxi is on the watch outside.

Water

In smooth waters — (*going easily*). They are passing a life in smooth waters.

In deep waters — (*in great difficulties*). They are passing their life in deep waters.

To throw cold water on — (*to discourage*). Please do not throw cold water on your son or else he will become a coward.

Blood is thicker than water — (*there is always a greater sympathy for a relative than for anyone else*).

Wax

Wax and wane — (*increase and decrease*). I have guts enough to stand in wax and wane.

Way

To go the way of the world — (*to die*). All of us have to go the way of the world one day.

Wear

Wear and tear — (*damage sustained as a result of ordinary use*). The wear and tear of an ordinary car is Rs. 200/- per month.

To wear well — (*to maintain youthful strength*). Even at the age of sixty he wears well.

To wear a principle in one's heart — (*be devoted to*). Vinobaji wears the principle of sympathy for poor in his heart.

Weather

To make the fair weather — (*to make the best of things*). Your brother is not intelligent enough to make the fair weather.

Wheel

Turn of wheel — (*change of fortune*). Just a little turn of wheel has made him a millionaire in two years.

To break on the wheel — (*to kill*). The thief broke on the wheel of the old man and ran away with five hundred rupees.

Wheel of life — (*vital processes*). One dies without the wheel of life.

Whip

To have the whiphand over — (*in a position to control*). The new teacher is having a whiphand over the naughty students.

Whirl

In a whirl — (*confusion*). He is in a whirl.

Whistle

Let go whistle (*disregard his wishes*). Unless you let go whistle you cannot do anything good for her.

Whistle down the winds — (*abandon*). In view of foreign exchange difficulties, the Government had to whistle down the wind of imports in the country.

Wind

To come from the four winds — (*to come from all sides*). We were caught in heavy rain when it came from the four winds last night.

Go like wind — (*swiftly*). An aeroplane always goes like wind.

Find out how the wind blows — (*what developments are likely*). Let us go and find out how the wind is blowing regarding the election of the president.

Wipe

Wipe out — (*destroy utterly*). The whole city has been wiped out by the earthquake.

To wipe one's eyes — (*to comfort*). Money wipes everybody's eyes.

Wish

If wishes were horses then beggers would ride — (*wishes alone cannot fulfil themselves*).

Wishful thinking — (*belief founded on wishes rather than facts*).

Wolf

A wolf in sheep's clothing — (*hypocrite*). A diplomat is a wolf in sheep's clothing.

Wonder

Signs of wonder — (*miracles*). If some signs of wonder happen, he may get through otherwise he has no chance.

Open-mouthed wonder — (*great surprise*). Your arrival is an open-mouthed wonder.

Word

A man of word — (*one who keeps promise*). He is a man of word.

Worm

To worm himself into another's favour — (*to get into a person's good graces through underhand means*).

Worst

If worse comes to worst — (*even under the worst result*).

Write

To write oneself out — (*to exhaust one's capacity to write*). He has now written himself out for the last few months.

Xanthic

Xanthic flowers — (*persons of everlasting beauty*). Her daughter is a xanthic flower.

Yarn

To spin a yarn — (*to tell tales*). Would you give up the habit of spinning a yarn ?

Year

Year by year — (*yearly*). We are making progress in our business year by year.

Young for one's years — (*bearing age lightly*). Your father looks young for his years.

Yellow

The yellow press — (*sensational newspapers*). A yellow press is a must for any modern country.

Yoke

Yoke of opinion — (*force of public opinion*). The Prime Minister was left with no choice except to accept yoke of opinion.

Young

Young things — (*young persons*). Young things should realize their responsibilities.

With young — (*pregnant*). Her mother is with young these days.

Z

A to Z

From A to Z — (*completely, thoroughly*). This departmental store sells A to Z consumer goods.

Zeal

With zest to zeal — (*with greater fervour*). The main quality in him is that he does everything with zest and zeal.

Zenith

To be at one's zenith — (*to be at the highest point of fame, glory, wealth, etc.*). Hema Malini is at her zenith now a days.

Zero

To become zero — (*to end in smoke*). Because of shortage of money all your plans have become zero.

Zest

To add zest to — (*to make interesting*). Unless the writer adds zest to his writing the readers will not buy his books.

Zig-Zag

Zig-zag — (*bent from side to side*). Life is always full of zig-zags.

NOTES

NOTES

NOTES